Ken Burtenshaw/Nik Mahon/Caroline Barfoot

The Fundamentals
of Creative
Advertising

ava | Academia
the environment of learning

Contents

The Fundamentals of Creative Advertising
Ken Burtenshaw/Nik Mahon/Caroline Barfoot

ava | Academia
the environment of learning

An AVA Book
Published by AVA Publishing SA
Rue des Fontenailles 16
Case Postale
1000 Lausanne 6
Switzerland
Tel: +41 786 005 109
Email: enquiries@avabooks.ch

Distributed by Thames & Hudson (ex-North America)
181a High Holborn
London WC1V 7QX
United Kingdom
Tel: +44 20 7845 5000
Fax: +44 20 7845 5055
Email: sales@thameshudson.co.uk
www.thamesandhudson.com

Distributed in the USA & Canada by:
Ingram Publishers Services Inc.
1 Ingram Blvd.
La Vergne, TN 37086
USA
Telephone: +1 866 400 5351
Fax: +1 800 838 1149
Email: customer.service@ingrampublisherservices.com

English Language Support Office
AVA Publishing (UK) Ltd.
Tel: +44 1903 204 455
Email: enquiries@avabooks.ch

ISBN 2-940373-18-3 and 978-2-940373-18-5

10 9 8 7 6 5 4 3

Cover design by Lucienne Roberts
Design by Gavin Ambrose
www.gavinambrose.co.uk
Project Editor: Lorna Fray
www.lornafray.co.uk

Production and separations by AVA Book
Production Pte. Ltd., Singapore
Tel: +65 6334 8173
Fax: +65 6259 9830
Email: production@avabooks.com.sg

How to get the most out of this book

The Fundamentals of Creative Advertising is an introduction to the important elements of the advertising process. It aims to give students a basic understanding of how advertising agencies create and produce advertising campaigns.

This book starts by introducing the modern advertising agency structure and the various media options available, outlining the pros and cons of each. The book then takes you through the process of planning, developing and executing an advertising campaign.

Finally, we assess the future direction of the advertising industry and list sources of further information to help you plan your career in advertising.

Explanatory text is backed up with numerous illustrations and photographs to represent examples of work from some of advertising's best practitioners. Related images that demonstrate the same point are captioned together.

Pierced (this page)
Ambient advertising is often opportunistic. This campaign for the Oslo Piercing Clinic used protruding fixtures on urban buildings and walls near the clinic, as part of the poster itself.

Client: Oslo Piercing Studio / Agency: Leo Burnett Oslo / Executive Creative Director: Erik Heisholt / Art Director: Erik Heisholt / Copywriter: Erik Heisholt, Marianne Heckmann, Per Erik Jarl

ForeheADS (opposite)
Cunning Stunts has developed a network of students to display brand logos or straplines on their foreheads. Ads are placed using a temporary transfer.

Agency: Cunning Stunts

Bus T-shirt (left)
This unusual D&z poster uses the space in a highly creative way.

Client: Procter and Gamble / Agency: Leo Burnett / Art Directors/Copywriters: Clark Edwards and Nick Pringle

The Economist (left)
Why not use the top of a bus as an advertising space? Now any urban space is fair game if it suits the product or brand. Here, *The Economist* says 'hello' to all its readers in high offices!

Client: *The Economist* / Agency: Abbott Mead Vickers BBDO Ltd. / Creative team: Malcolm Duffy and Paul Briginshaw

Advantages of the medium
- Posters can be produced in various sizes and shapes, which offers the creative team a greater variety of creative opportunities.
- Posters can be three-dimensional, which also opens up new creative possibilities.
- The audience passing the site may read the message again and again on a daily basis.
- Sites can be bought close to the point of purchase (where the product is on sale).
- Posters are an effective way of building awareness for the brand over time.
- Flexible timing: individual sites and packages can be purchased for as little as two weeks up to 12 months and copy can be changed on a monthly basis.
- Regionally flexible: individual sites and packages can be bought within television regions, conurbations, towns or smaller, targeted environments (maybe even outside competitors' offices!).

Disadvantages of the medium
- Some sites can be vandalised or posters sprayed with graffiti.
- Posting can be unreliable (e.g. time-sensitive posters may not be posted on time).
- Site rental can be expensive.
- It is difficult to reach a national audience through posters, especially when compared with other media such as national press and consumer magazines.
- Prime locations can be tied up in long-term contracts, giving you limited availability.

Creating a more effective poster
Here are few pointers to creating better poster advertising:
- Your poster must be memorable and convey the message effectively.
- It must be visible above the street clutter.
- Remember the passer-by only has a few seconds to register the message before switching off, so your poster needs to stand out from its surroundings – it needs to be eye-catching.
- Keep the visual simple – the iPod poster imagery is a classic example. Consider using a single image.
- Don't write a headline with more than seven or eight words!
- Make the type as legible as possible. This may mean using strong, bold typefaces. This will improve the clarity of the communication. Sans serif typefaces such as Helvetica, Franklin Gothic and Grotesque are very effective.
- Cut out clutter in your layout. If you manage with just a headline, great.
- Make the branding strong. This applies to all media; the advertisement should evoke the brand – which doesn't just mean having a big logo.

Do it!

Each section concludes with a 'Do it!' exercise, which is an opportunity for you to put the theory into practice and to hone your creative skills.

Key information is featured in box outs or diagrams, for clarity.

The client

Most advertising campaigns are created by an agency, working on behalf of an organisation, corporation, manufacturer or individual; in all cases the 'client'. Few clients choose to handle their advertising internally, or 'in-house', as most appreciate that commissioning an agency can bring fresh ideas and objectivity to the job in hand.

In many ways the relationship between the client and the agency is mutually beneficial, but ultimately it is the client that controls the budget and can elect to move their account at any time. The agency's fear that an account might be moved can lead to their agreeing to a campaign strategy that they may not be entirely happy with, simply to accommodate the client's wishes. In such cases the results are often disastrous and the relationship between both parties can be irreparably damaged, as both parties blame each other for the failure of the campaign. The 'fear factor' still exists, but these days the relationship between the agency and the client tends to be built on a greater sense of partnership. Most major clients have learned to trust the judgement of their agencies and agencies have learned to involve the client in key stages of the process.

The client brief
Once the relationship between the client and agency is established, work on a campaign can begin. Every project starts with a brief from the client. This brief is usually in the form of a written document, which is then presented verbally to the agency. The client brief should clearly state the objectives of the campaign, based on a thorough analysis of the current status of the brand and its marketplace. The client brief shouldn't tell the agency how to do their job, but it should give them as much guidance and information as possible to help them arrive at the best solution.

Structuring the client brief
The British Institute of Practitioners in Advertising recently put together a best practice guide on behalf of a number of industry bodies (*The Client Brief*, 2003, IPA, London. Copies are available from www.ipa.org.uk). The guide includes a comprehensive list of what should be included in a client brief and communicated to an agency.

Essentials for a client brief
- Where are we now?
- Where do we want to be?
- What are we doing to get there?
- Who do we need to talk to?
- How will we know when we've arrived?
- Practicalities
- Approvals

Where are we now?
Firstly the client brief should detail the current position of the brand, product or service in terms of sales, market share, distribution, and consumer attitudes. The client must be completely honest about the brand/product/service and present its weaknesses as well as its strengths. It is also important for the brief to recognise any threats posed by competitors as well as any opportunities that are yet to be exploited.

A SWOT (Strengths, Weaknesses, Opportunities and Threats) analysis is a useful tool that allows the client to display the brand in the context of the marketplace which it operates in – see the example shown below.

Strengths
Examples of the brand's strong points in the marketplace. These are often compared to competitors, e.g. market leader.

Weaknesses
Any problems that the brand is facing. Might include issues such as consumers no longer finding the brand relevant or the fact that the product doesn't offer the same benefits as its competitors.

Opportunities
These might include the opportunity to market the brand to a new target audience or a change in legislation such as the inclusion of new member states into the EU.

Threats
The threat may come from a new competitor entering the marketplace or a change in legislation that may limit the marketing opportunities of the brand, e.g. potential restrictions on advertising to children and health issues such as Bird Flu.

Introduction

THE END OF THE QUESTION MARK. Text any question to 83336 and have the answer within minutes.

We set out to write a book that explains the fundamentals of creative advertising and follows one of the great adages of advertising; 'keep it simple'. Written in plain English and as jargon free as possible, this book contains visual examples of some of the best 'creative advertising' around, from recent times and past years. These examples play an important part in illustrating the concepts and approaches covered within this book, and will hopefully inspire your own creativity.

The main purpose of this book is to give you a basic understanding of how creative advertising campaigns are planned and created. This is achieved by focusing on the advertising techniques and approaches practised by modern advertising agencies. A special emphasis is placed on exploring the role of creative teams employed by these agencies to conceive ideas, and their involvement in the evolution of advertising campaigns. Relevant examples, together with comments from advertising practitioners, supplement the text.

We have also included practical student exercises at the end of some sections. These are designed to apply information from the various sections and help you to build a strong and professional portfolio of creative work.

Firstly, it is important to set the scene by understanding some basic background information about how advertising agencies are structured and how they function. This book concentrates on the working practices of full-service agencies, where all the client's communication requirements are met under one roof.

For many clients it makes sense to have continuity across an advertising campaign and to use a single agency for the whole of that campaign. This means that communication lines are straightforward and any potential misunderstandings can be avoided. However, some clients prefer the idea of hiring specialists in various fields from different agencies. This can often give the client greater flexibility and freedom to choose specialists on the basis of their creative strengths, experience and suitability for the task. Some advertising agencies specialise in direct marketing, sales promotion and sponsorship and some specialise in business areas such as business-to-business, corporate, pharmaceutical and recruitment.

One area of advertising specialisation is the task of concept generation itself. This has been reflected by an increase in creative boutiques or 'hot shops', whose strength is to turn out highly creative work quickly – without being hindered by the complex infrastructure or bureaucracy of larger agencies. These small agencies are run by advertising creatives, normally

creative directors, who have often broken away from more established agencies to concentrate purely on the creative product. They are sometimes used to add a fresh and different approach to projects and have the advantage of dealing direct with the client rather than communicating via account handlers.

New wave advertising agencies, such as Mother and St. Lukes, have evolved over the past ten years into egalitarian organisations. The St. Lukes agency, where none of the staff have an office and everyone is a co-owner, was voted agency of the year in the UK in its second year. The agency's website gives an insight into their 'different' company philosophy:

'Our people work in cross-disciplined teams rather than in departments. Our systems, our processes and our environment have been configured to place creativity and our clients' business at the heart of our business.'

This focus on the client is taken a stage further at St. Lukes with the creation of brand rooms, where the furnishing, fittings and decoration are designed around the client's business. This client-centred approach creates agency headquarters for all activities on the account.

With its emphasis on the creative aspects of advertising, this book provides an overview of current practices, organisational models and media options, together with references to both traditional and contemporary views and approaches.

Illustrations (opposite and above)

A huge number of ads and creative concepts are reproduced in this book to illustrate the text, represent the variety of creative advertising and hopefully inspire you.

Full details and credits for these images are on pages 125 and 139 respectively.

The agency structure

Although new wave agencies have prospered, the traditional full-service agencies are still responsible for producing some of the best creative advertising. They are normally structured around five key departments or sections.

Account management

The account executive and manager/supervisor liaise on a regular basis between the agency and the client. Once the strategic plan and campaign guidelines have been agreed with the client, the account team is there to supervise and administer them. They then project manage the various advertising campaigns, liaising with individuals and teams in other agency departments. The account team is also responsible for pursuing and securing new business and the organisation of any 'pitches' (new business presentations).

Account planning

Planning involves having a clear understanding and profile of the consumer or customer and their potential relationship with the brand. Understanding their perspective, habits, needs and buying behaviour is important to the development of a strong strategic plan. This involves using various forms of qualitative market research, including focus groups and interviews. The planner and the creative team tend to work closely on the development of the creative brief.

Media planning and buying

Here, media specialists plan the most efficient (and cost effective) way of delivering the advertising concept to the target audience. In their own way they can be extremely creative – they find new and exciting media opportunities to expose advertising messages. It is also important that they negotiate the best spots (time slots), spaces and prices for advertisements in various media. They deal with newspapers, magazines and TV companies on a daily basis to achieve the best deals.

The creative department

Creative teams usually work in pairs under the guidance of the creative director, the person with overall responsibility for an agency's creative output. Creative teams are responsible for the origination of advertising ideas and concepts from a creative brief supplied by the account team. Traditionally the team was made up of an art director and copywriter, however in reality the division of labour is blurred – the art director is just as likely to think up a headline as the copywriter will the visual! Once the client has approved the campaign idea, the creative team follows the idea through to the final execution.

The production department

Once a creative concept has been approved, it's up to the production department to turn the idea into reality in whatever format is required. They will work closely with the art director to make sure that their interpretation is right and that the campaign looks exactly as it was meant to. The production manager will often use outside companies such as TV production companies and poster print specialists – one of their key roles is finding the right company to do the job at the right price. This can mean working with purchasing teams from the client, as they may have a list of approved suppliers that they want to work with. Working in the production department is very high pressure, as you are always working to close deadlines and if someone doesn't deliver on time it's the production department who will be blamed for the delay.

In an industry where rapid advances in technology are driving change at an equally rapid pace, it is perhaps the need for creativity, and individuals who can think creatively, that remains the only constant in all of this. The capacity to have original ideas, and apply those ideas to woo audiences in a persuasive and compelling way, will remain at the hub of every great advertising campaign.

The client

Account team
Account director
Account manager
Account executive

Account planning

Creative department

Media buying and planning

Production department

CHAPTER 1
THE MEDIA OPTIONS

Posters

In the 1970s UK advertising agencies, led by the legendary Collett, Dickenson and Pearce (CDP), were instrumental in popularising 48 and 96-sheet posters with clients. Award-winning posters, such as those for Walls sausages and Parker pens, revitalised a poster industry that had suffered in the previous 20 years from the impact of commercial television. The success of these posters lay in the simplicity of both their message and their visual.

The poster medium dictates that advertisements communicate their message, within a matter of seconds, to an audience of busy passers-by. Consequently, the creative teams behind poster advertisements often use short, sometimes witty headlines coupled with punchy, eye-catching visuals to 'shout' a simple and undiluted message to their audience. In the UK, posters are made up of 'sheets' (either 32, 48 or 96 sheets as standard), while in Europe they are measured in square metres.

Posters offer advertisers a host of opportunities and are a powerful, highly visible and cost effective means of communication. Also referred to as 'outdoor' advertising, the poster is a medium that can be used in different environments or locations and in a variety of shapes and sizes. As such, posters have become an integral part of the cityscape and unlike other media, such as television and press advertising, posters need only the street to exist – fly posters stand side by side with 48 and 96 sheet posters.

Ever since poster makers like Cheret and Toulouse Lautrec launched their colourful lithographic artwork on to the streets of Paris in the late nineteenth century, the poster has proved to be a popular means of advertising. Pears Soap and later Guinness continued the tradition, each creating timeless posters. For example, from the early 1930s through to the 1950s, John Gilroy was responsible for creating posters which included phrases such as 'Guinness for Strength', 'It's a Lovely Day for a Guinness' and, most famously, 'My Goodness – My Guinness'. The posters featured Gilroy's distinctive artwork and more often than not featured animals such as a kangaroo, ostrich, seal, lion, and notably a toucan, which subsequently became as much a symbol of Guinness as the harp.
The poster has remained a constant medium, with the ability to communicate with broad audiences in a language that they understand.

Would you be more careful if it was you that got pregnant?

Anyone married or single can get advice on contraception from the Family Planning Association
Margaret Pyke House, 27-35 Mortimer Street, London W1 N 8BQ. Tel. 01-636 9135.

The Health Education Council

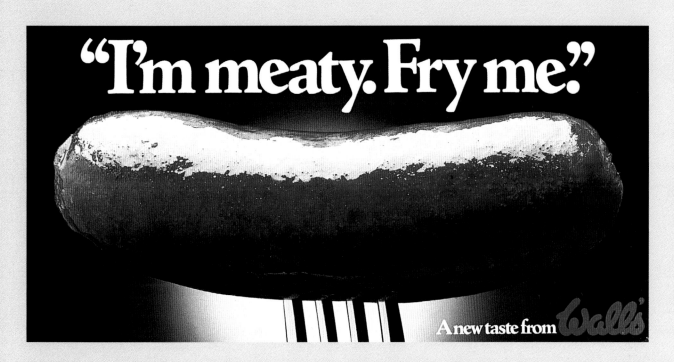

Pregnant man (opposite)

The combination of words and picture communicate the message simply and directly.

Client: Health Education Council (UK) / Agency: Saatchi & Saatchi / Art Director: Bill Atherton / Copywriter: Jeremy Sinclair / Photographer: Alan Brooking. Reproduced under the terms of the Click-Use Licence

'I'm meaty. Fry me.' (above)

This famous CDP poster parodied the British Airways ads of the day.

Client: Walls / Agency: CDP / Copywriter: Terry Lovecock / Art Director: Paul Smith / Photographer: Ed White (Image used with kind permission of CDP-Travissully)

Roseanne Holland (below)

This tragic series of photographs, incorporated into a 48-sheet poster, demonstrates the power of showing real images in an ad campaign.

Client: Metropolitan Police / Agency: Miles Calcraft Briginshaw Duffy / Creative Directors: Paul Briginshaw and Malcolm Duffy / Art Director and Copywriter: Jeremy Carr

Sheep. Video. (above and above left)

This campaign for Carling Extra Cold features a series of quirky images that use black humour to good effect.

Client: Leith London / Agency: Leith London / Art Director: John Messum / Copywriter: Simon Bere

DON'T LET DRUG DEALERS CHANGE THE FACE OF YOUR NEIGHBOURHOOD.
Call Crimestoppers anonymously on 0800 555 111.

The Economist (this page)

The long-running poster campaign for *The Economist* effortlessly demonstrates the skills of communicating a simple yet clever message to a discerning audience, who they appear to know very well (below). The use of a simple trademark red background, and white out lettering for the magazine's name and clever headlines, make these posters stand out on the street. In later campaigns (above and right), posters started using visuals associated with intelligence and bright thinking instead of a headline.

Client: *The Economist* / Agency: Abbott Mead Vickers BBDO Limited /
Lightbulb: Art Director: Paul Belford / Writer: Nigel Roberts
Brains: Art Director: Tony Hardcastle / Writer: Mark Tweddell
Would you like to sit next to you at dinner?: Art Director: Ron Brown /
Copywriter: David Abbott

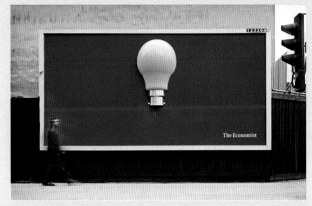

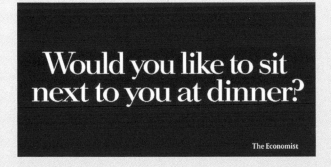

How did it come to this?

Michael Jackson's Face | Sun 29th Sept 9pm | **see five**

If this is what's happening outside, what's going on inside?

Michael Jackson's Face | Sun 29th Sept 9pm | **see five**

Michael Jackson's face (opposite)

This poster took up an entire wall on an underground train platform at
Leicester Square station, London.

Client: Channel Five / Agency: TBWA London / Creative Director: Trevor
Beattie / Art Director: Bill Bungay

Sch... you know who? (above)

Photographer Alison Jackson's celebrity lookalike photographs were used
to produce this award-winning poster campaign.

Client: Schweppes/The Coca Cola Company / Agency: Mother / Creative
Director: Robert Saville / Art Directors and Copywriters: Caroline Pay, Kim
Gehrig / Photographer: Alison Jackson

Right space, right location

The success of any poster campaign depends not only on the quality of the creative idea and its ability to engage with the target audience, but also the appropriateness of the media planning and buying. Gaining an appreciation of the right space and the right location for the message to be seen by the target audience is crucial. Although many agencies have specialist media planners, whose job is to schedule and eventually buy the media for the advertising campaign, it is important not to divorce yourself from this process as the location can be instrumental in influencing the direction of your creative concept. For example, if your brief was to advertise a new brand of fruit drink by poster, where would your posters be best situated? Logically, posters close to supermarkets, high streets or shopping malls 'talk' to potential consumers, as they are often travelling to a shop. Colin Stone, a media-planning specialist with 25 years experience, expands on this point.

'Clever planning and buying of selected sites can be achieved to reach important target groups, such as airports for frequent travellers, club and business class lounges for businessmen and health clubs for young executives. Individual site selection (line by line) requires detailed local knowledge to avoid pitfalls. Most poster contractors will attempt to package sites and sell them at a perceived discount, but this rarely allows any chance for quality control or inspection until after the campaign is over. Pre- and post-awareness research can also be implemented and provides a good idea of whether the message is being seen.'

Giant posters and special builds

There are abundant creative poster opportunities available to advertising teams. Poster sites and street furniture can be designed and commissioned to suit the needs of the poster design or campaign idea (see Ambient media, p.28).

Specially designed and built posters, such as three-dimensional giant Marlboro men protruding from the Hollywood hillside or cars stuck to billboards along the roadside, have been a feature of the American urban landscape for decades. And because posters are a big advertising medium, some sites have grown in size through the sheer opportunism of the advertiser – sides of buildings in construction or multi-storey car parks are all fair game. Although giving the brand name exposure is undoubtedly one of the most important functions of poster advertising, the 'big is beautiful' philosophy can sometimes lead to crude branding that lacks any central creative, campaignable idea.

Perfect day (below)
This panoramic landscape photograph of Scotland is ideally suited for this poster, which was situated on the concourse of a major railway station.

Client: Visit Scotland / Agency: 1576 / Art Director: Brian McGregor / Copywriter: Adrian Jeffery / Photographer: Paul Tompkins

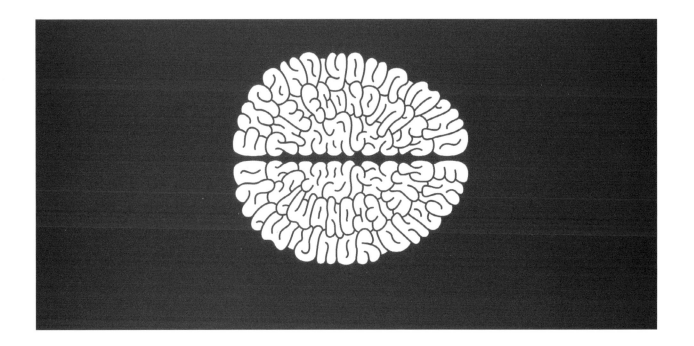

Sheep (below)

This long-running, giant poster campaign demonstrates the value of sticking with a strong, campaignable idea.

Client: Castlemaine XXXX / Agency: Bartle Bogle Hegarty UK / Producer: Dave Robinson/Paul Stacy / Photographer: Simon Stock / Creative Team: John O'Keeffe, Jon Fox, Rik Brown

The Economist (above)

The use of visuals has successfully moved *The Economist* 's expand your mind campaign on to another level.

Client: *The Economist* / Agency: Abbott Mead Vickers BBDO Limited / Art Director: Paul Belford / Copywriter: Nigel Roberts / Illustrator: Paul Belford / Typographer: John Tisdall

**Benson and Hedges
(this page)**

The famous and innovative Benson
and Hedges posters appeared in
the late 1970s and featured
surreal, visual puzzles. This was
cigarette advertising that featured
no copy apart from a health
warning, which advised us to the
dangers of smoking.

Client: Benson and Hedges
Agency: CDP / Creative team: Mike
Cozens and Alan Waldie /
Photographer: Brian Duffy
(Image used with kind permission
of CDP-Travissully)

Public transport advertising

Not all outdoor advertising needs to capture audience attention in the same way. Sometimes the advertiser has the time to talk to a captive audience – either waiting for transport or already on their journey – if they impart their message on a poster displayed at a station, on a train, in a taxi or even on the back of a seat.

According to research carried out by Viacom Outdoor, a leading transport media sales company, the average London Underground train passenger spends approximately three minutes on the platform waiting for their train. Large, cross tracks underground posters afford the opportunity for advertisers to entertain, by use of witty, clever headlines and visuals, and there is even the time for their audience to read any supporting body copy about the product or service. This captive audience time even gives the creative team the chance to set puzzles and conundrums, which creates an interaction with the waiting passenger and potential consumer.

Public transport advertising also gives the creative team an opportunity to link their idea directly to the context and experience of travelling on a particular type of transport. Consider for example the case of tube cards (landscape posters inside underground train carriages) and escalator panels (small posters that run alongside escalators). In city centres across Europe (and more recently in the UK), trams are a popular mode of transport and advertisers use the inside and outside of carriages as another advertising opportunity.

Rail advertising offers an opportunity to reach a broad audience, from upmarket daily business commuters, to leisure travellers, who all have a relatively long time to dwell on their surroundings. Train stations also offer the advertiser the chance to connect with niche markets, such as people travelling to a particular venue for a specific exhibition or event. As a creative it is important to be aware of significant dates in the calendar, especially ones that may be relevant to the brands you are working on. For example if the client is a confectionery manufacture or supplier of flowers then something like Mother's Day will create a wealth of opportunity.

The advertiser has long seen bus advertising as a means of carrying simple brand messages to target groups and offering a point-of-sale prompt – advertisements on buses are travelling billboards speaking directly to consumers on their journey to a shopping environment. Similarly, posters placed on the back of buses can talk to other road users in their own environment – products such as car insurance or breakdown services would be well placed here. For the creative team, buses offer another, larger canvas to show off their ideas. The T-shape poster format allows for the use of headlines and landscape visuals that span the side of the bus. Some have gone even further and decorated the whole bus.

A: Because the first bus has more passengers to pick up than the second, and the second more than the third – this tends to reduce the intervals between them

Notes and Queries
Every Wednesday
The Guardian

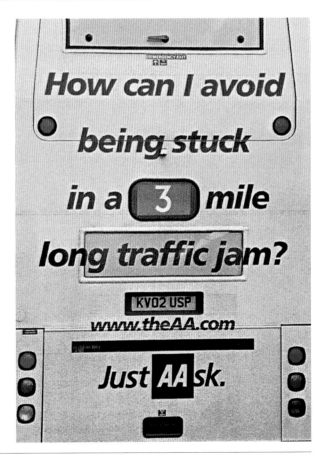

How can I avoid being stuck in a 3 mile long traffic jam?

KV02 USP

www.theAA.com

Just AAsk.

Notes and queries. Traffic jam. (this page)

Buses offer the creative team a moving poster site, delivering its message across a town or city.

Notes and queries: Client: *The Guardian* / Agency: DBB / Art Director: Nick Allsop / Copywriter: Simon Veksner / Typographer: Peter Mould
Traffic jam: Client: The Automoblie Association / Agency: M&C Saatchi / Art Director: Simon Dicketts / Typography: Rob Wilson

Meet today's underground filmmakers (opposite)

Channel 4 television ran a truly innovative advertising campaign to promote its broadband documentary channel, FourDocs. Installations at railway stations and cinemas enabled members of the public to download short video documentaries directly to their mobile phone via Bluetooth. The campaign was cutting-edge and ambitious, reflecting the channel's brand and the nature of the advertised service – a website for sharing short documentaries.

Client: Channel 4 / Concept: Tracy Blacher and Steve Forde, Channel 4 Marketing / Online creative: Florian Schmitt, Hi-Res! / Offline creative: Jane Smillie, 4Creative / Media planning and buying: Lindsay Green, consultant, Jonny Mackay, OMD
(Image reproduced courtesy of Viacom Outdoor and photographer Rosie Mayell)

Bus T-shirt (left)

This unusual Daz poster uses the space in a highly creative way.

Client: Proctor and Gamble / Agency: Leo Burnett / Art Directors/Copywriters: Clark Edwards and Nick Pringle

The Economist (left)

Why not use the top of a bus as an advertising space? Now any urban space is fair game if it suits the product or brand. Here, *The Economist* says 'hello' to all its readers in high office!

Client: *The Economist* / Agency: Abbott Mead Vickers BBDO Ltd. / Creative team: Malcolm Duffy and Paul Briginshaw

Advantages of the medium

- Posters can be produced in various sizes and shapes, which offers the creative team a greater variety of creative opportunities.
- Posters can be three-dimensional, which also opens up new creative possibilities.
- The audience passing the site may read the message again and again on a daily basis.
- Sites can be bought close to the point of purchase (where the product is on sale).
- Posters are an effective way of building awareness for the brand over time.
- Flexible timing: individual sites and packages can be purchased for as little as two weeks up to 12 months and copy can be changed on a monthly basis.
- Regionally flexible: individual sites and packages can be bought within television regions, conurbations, towns or smaller, targeted environments (maybe even outside competitors' offices!).

Disadvantages of the medium

- Some sites can be vandalised or posters sprayed with graffiti.
- Posting can be unreliable (e.g. time-sensitive posters may not be posted on time).
- Site rental can be expensive.
- It is difficult to reach a national audience through posters, especially when compared with other media such as national press and consumer magazines.
- Prime locations can be tied up in long-term contracts, giving you limited availability.

Creating a more effective poster

Here are few pointers to creating better poster advertising:

- Your poster must be memorable and convey the message effectively.
- It must be visible above the street clutter.
- Remember the passer-by only has a few seconds to register the message before switching off, so your poster needs to stand out from its surroundings – it needs to be eye-catching.
- Keep the visual simple – the iPod poster imagery is a classic example. Consider using a single image.
- Don't write a headline with more than seven or eight words!
- Make the type as legible as possible. This may mean using strong, bold typefaces. This will improve the clarity of the communication. Sans serif typefaces such as Helvetica, Franklin Gothic and Grotesque are very effective.
- Cut out clutter in your layout. If you manage with just a headline, great.
- Make the branding strong. This applies to all media; the advertisement should evoke the brand – which doesn't just mean having a big logo.

Do it!

Produce a series of tube or metro posters to advertise extra strong peppermints. The proposition for these mints is that they give you 'fresh breath confidence'. Remember that the context of the communication's location can affect your idea. The people travelling on the tube/metro are obviously keen to smell their very best, so play on this.

To trigger off some initial ideas, try producing a list of key words/phrases associated with travelling on the tube – ticket, zones, tube line names, 'mind the doors' and so on. It is amazing how many good ideas start this way! Then try the same process from another angle – 'crowded carriage, people are too close', 'stop treading on my toe', 'I can smell garlic' etc. Remember that you are talking to people who have some time to read your message – they may be on the train for several stops, so you may be able to tell a short story.

Ambient media

Ambient media is a relatively new phenomenon in terms of advertising, so-called because it is advertising that is in keeping with, or becomes part of, the environment that the target audience is likely to encounter. Ambient media tends to occupy an area between advertising and promotional stunts, and can, in many cases, involve relatively little expenditure. In an age where the consumer tends to be wary of the 'hard sell' and constant exposure to advertising and promotion, the use of original and unexpected media such as this can be very effective precisely because it often allows the message to slip beneath the 'consumer radar'. The best ambient campaigns put the media at the centre of the communication, in a way that is often unconventional, yet relevant to the advertising message.

There is a wide range of objects, items and fixtures that can fall within the realm of ambient media, such as beer mats, carrier bags, bus and train tickets, video screens, litter bins, floors and paving, take-away drink lids, payroll statements, shopping trolleys and ashtrays. Advertisers are constantly seeking fresh, innovative ways to communicate their message and this frequently involves the use of quirkier and more unusual forms of ambient media.

Ice car (above)
This exact replica of a Polo Twist sculpted entirely from ice was left in a busy London street. It is an unusual ambient idea that promotes the air conditioning features of the car in a publicity-catching way.

Client: Volkswagen UK / Agency: DDB London / Art Directors: Gavin Siakimotu and Graeme Hall / Copywriters: Graeme Hall and Gavin Siakimotu / Creative Directors: Jeremy Craigen and Ewan Paterson
(Image supplied courtesy of the D&AD Global Awards (Ambient media: Silver nomination, 2005))

Womankind bus stop and crime scene sign (this page)
Low cost ambient media 'stunts' such as these work really well for charity clients. They also generate publicity and public interest.

Client: Womankind / Agency: Rainey Kelly Campbell Roalfe/Y&R /
Art Director: Jerry Hollens / Copywriter: Mike Boles

Try an easier way in (this page and opposite)
This week-long ambient stunt was aimed at creating awareness among City of London financial workers of the career possibilities at The Royal Bank of Scotland. The 'try an easier way in' web-driven campaign asked people to view the career opportunities on the bank's website.

Client: The Royal Bank of Scotland Group / Agency: TMP Worldwide / Creative Directors: Giles Ecott and Roger Cayless / Creative team: Ricky Nordson and Richard Nott

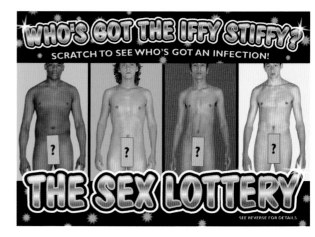

Sex lottery (this page)

To raise awareness about the risks of sexually transmitted infections, Delaney Lund Knox Warren & Partners created an ambient campaign involving the use of lottery style scratchcards. The 'Sex lottery' scratchcards were distributed in clubs, bars and anywhere else that a youth audience was likely to be found. Recipients would scratch off the patches on the surface of each card to find out what sexually transmitted infections they could catch. The slogan: 'Don't play the sex lottery. Use a condom' accompanied the campaign.

Client: Department of Health/COI (UK) / Agency: Delaney Lund Knox Warren & Partners / Art Director: Ken Sara / Copywriter: Jon Elsom

Tree labels (opposite)

This ambient campaign for Glenbrook Bonsai Nursery uses a mixture of humour, irony and pastiche in the way giant-sized plant labels are tied around full-sized living trees.

Client: Glenbrook Bonsai Nursery / Agency: McCann-Erickson Bristol / Creative Director: David Woolway / Art Director: Stuart Richings / Copywriter: Stuart Richings / Typographer: Chris Wigmore

The rise of ambient media

Ambient media provides advertisers with an alternative to traditional (and often more expensive) forms of advertising, which are often readily bypassed by consumers. The potential of ambient media as part of a larger multimedia campaign has been recognised by many of the world's leading brands, and research indicates that it is currently the fastest growing advertising media sector.

Some of the earliest examples of ambient media include beer mats in pubs and bars, the sides of taxis and fuel pumps at service stations. Although consumers were familiar with these items as functional utilities, at the time few had encountered them as an advertising medium. Many of these early forms of ambient media have now become so commonplace that the 'surprise effect' has diminished. Advertisers are constantly seeking new and unusual media to convey their message and this has led to some very imaginative and original solutions. For example, DARG, an animal rescue organisation based on the outskirts of Cape Town, South Africa managed to persuade all of the one hour photo-laboratories in the area to insert photographs of the dogs that DARG were hoping to find homes for, inside the packs of customers' photographs that were ready for collection. The photographs were printed in the same format as the customers' own snapshots and carried the copy line: 'he looks like part of the family already' on the reverse side, together with the organisation's contact details.

The real strength of ambient media lies in its ability to take the consumer by surprise. It presents consumers with the advertising message when they least expect it. This not only makes the message hard to avoid, but it can also make it more memorable. Its location is of prime importance – one aspect common to most ambient media campaigns is that they use or react with the attributes of the immediate environment in which they are placed, to such an extent that the environment often becomes part of the advertisement too. In many cases this placement of ambient advertisements is witty as well as clever. Bars, clubs and leisure centres can be a great environment for ambient media because they provide an opportunity to catch people when their guard is down.

We have also become a vehicle for the advertising message with the brands we wear and the logos we carry on our T-shirts, hats, shoes, sportswear and carrier bags. Agencies are already beginning to use volunteers' bodies as an advertising medium – shaved heads, bare stomachs, arms and legs provide an irresistible tool for future advertisers to present a sales message in an attention grabbing way.

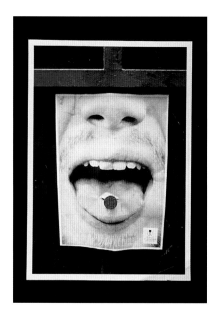 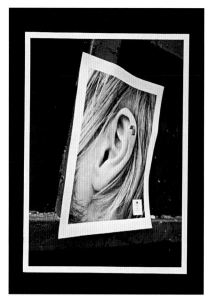 

Pierced (this page)

Ambient advertising is often opportunistic. This campaign for the Oslo Piercing Clinic used protruding fixtures on urban buildings and walls near the clinic, as part of the poster itself.

Client: Oslo Piercing Studio / Agency: Leo Burnett Oslo / Executive Creative Director: Erik Heisholt / Art Director: Erik Heisholt / Copywriter: Erik Heisholt, Marianne Heckmann, Per Erik Jarl

ForeheADS (opposite)

Cunning Stunts has developed a network of students to display brand logos or straplines on their foreheads. Ads are placed using a temporary transfer.

Agency: Cunning Stunts

FIND A LICENSED MINICAB ANYWHERE
IN THE UK FROM YOUR MOBILE OR PC

SIMPLY text "taxi" followed by a space and the...............................
postcode you are travelling from e.g. "taxi SW11" to..............................
60040.......and for 50p ....
we'll text back the numbers of 3 local..
licensed cab operators ....
Or do it online at .... **cabnumbers**.com

PO Box 42925, London SW12 0XE

BE SAFE & ALWAYS CARRY THIS CARD WITH YOU

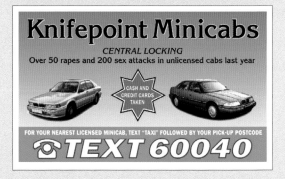

Taxi cards (this page)

These taxi cards were dropped in selected areas of London to alert people to the perils of travelling in an unlicensed taxi. Once again, pastiche design helps to enhance the 'surprise' element, while strong headlines combined with shocking facts and statistics, help drive the message home.

Client: cardnumbers.com / Agency: M&C Saatchi / Art Directors and Copywriters: Tom Spicer and Sergio Martin / Typographer: Simon Warden

Stamp (left)

50 rubber handstamps were produced (in the style of those used to prove paid entry to music gigs) to create awareness of *The Guardian*'s free CD offer. Those who had been 'stamped' on Friday evening woke on Saturday morning to find the message still visible on the back of their hand.

Client: *The Guardian* / Agency: Claydon Heeley / Creative Directors: Dave Woods and Pete Harle / Art Director: Nick Thompson / Copywriter: Josh Haines

MPV towcar (right)

A Renault Espace MPV towed this mobile poster trailer around London streets to demonstrate its award winning towing capability.

Client: Renault / Agency: Publicis UK / Art Director: Cameron Blackley / Copywriter: Andrew Petch / Photographer: Julian Wolkenstein / Production Manager: Steve McFarlane

Guerrilla advertising

'Guerrilla' advertising is a term used to describe campaigns that create a 'buzz' or generate discussion or debate via the use of non-traditional methods in highly unexpected and attention-grabbing ways.

The medium used in guerrilla campaigns is often ambient as the environment around the advertisement can play a major role in conveying the message. Guerrilla campaigns catch their audience unaware, in fact the term 'guerrilla' takes on a special significance here as the audience is literally 'ambushed' by the advertising message. The nature of the advertising message in guerrilla campaigns is often hidden or disguised. In most cases, the target audience is completely unaware that they are being confronted by advertising, and in cases where they eventually become aware; the message has already been absorbed. Guerrilla marketing tactics can extend the strategic impact and effectiveness of an advertising campaign.

Guerrilla advertising campaigns can combine a variety of tactics including fly posters, stickers, ambient media or creative and publicity-grabbing stunts. For example the opening of the Hard Rock Hotel in Chicago, USA was accompanied by a campaign that involved models, dressed in bathrobes, walking the streets nearby to the hotel. The models were instructed to ask passers-by for directions back to the hotel, explaining that they had attended a party there the night before and got lost when they had left to get some fresh air.

Viral advertising is a guerrilla tactic involving the communication of advertising messages from person-to-person by email (see Online advertising p.64).

'art-ilisers' posters (this page)

Britart.com appointed Mother to help establish them as the world's largest internet art gallery. In a departure from the more traditional forms of advertising commonly used by galleries, Mother created a guerrilla advertising campaign that involved the creation of 'art-ilisers': pastiche labels identifying works of art. These were printed large scale as fly posters, which were then strategically placed in outdoor locations thus turning street furniture into art. A second wave of the campaign created office art-ilisers, which identified everyday office items as art, and a third wave focused on 'art-ilising' objects around the home.

Client: Britart.com / Agency: Mother / Art Directors and Copywriters: Cecilia Dufils, Markus Bjurman, Kim Gehrig and Joe de Souza

Advantages of the medium

- Ambient media takes the audience by surprise, it slips 'under the radar' and gets its message across before it's recognised as an advertisement.
- It tends to generate a 'buzz' and get people talking.
- Ambient media can often generate extra media coverage in newspapers or television/radio news reports.
- Ambient media is often more dramatic and novel in the way it is presented. This makes it stand out from more traditional forms of advertising.
- The dramatic and often unconventional use of media makes the advertisement more memorable.
- Ambient media can be relatively cheap to use compared with more traditional forms of advertising media.

Disadvantages of the medium

- A lot of ambient media campaigns are 'one-off' stunts and offer fleeting moments of exposure.
- Many ambient campaigns or stunts court controversy, and can in some extreme cases prompt complaints from the general public.
- Audience coverage can be limited. Some of the more elaborate ambient campaigns or guerrilla stunts are difficult to transport on a wide geographic scale to a larger number of locations. In such cases, the campaign will rely on extra media coverage by newspapers, TV and radio news programmes etc., to reach a wider audience.
- Ambient campaigns may not always 'fit' well with the advertiser's current house style or existing advertising campaign.

Do it!

Use ambient media to sell yourself! Think ahead to the prospect of finding a job in advertising. To get that important foot in the door you need to stand out from the competition. A strong portfolio of ideas and a great personality are important, but you may need something else to give you the edge.

Create an ambient campaign that promotes your skills or field of expertise. This is likely to have more impact than just a CV with a business card and a covering letter.

Think about who you are targeting. What places do they frequent? Where can you take them by surprise? Once you've considered all the potential media sites (indoor and outdoor), think of how you could use aspects or elements of that environment as part of the media itself.

Newspapers and magazines

Press and magazine advertisements offer the agency a great opportunity to flex their creative muscles. As with many advertising media, the creative team must quickly persuade their audience to notice and then read their advertisement in newspapers or magazines – failing to command the reader's attention will mean that the page will be turned or the reader's eye will be drawn to something else. Traditionally the combination of headline, visual, body copy, strapline and brand name makes this medium different from posters. Also the reader is sitting at home, on the bus or train reading the newspaper or magazine, not rushing past a poster site on their way to work or to the supermarket.

Anatomy of a press/magazine advertisement

Although there is no set formula that can be applied to create a successful print advertisement, creative teams have traditionally combined a punchy headline with a complementary visual to attract the reader's attention and then lead them directly to the advertisement's body copy. When writing a headline, the copywriter can use interesting facts or trivia to grab reader attention or create intrigue about the advertisement. The body copy then allows the copywriter to present the product or brand's selling features. This is usually followed by a brand logo, a slogan or strapline and the organisation's or manufacturer's contact details (see Copywriting, p.106).

David Abbott, copywriter and co-author of *The Copywriter's Bible*, perfected the art of writing press advertising copy by writing intriguing and teasing headlines that led the reader into the body text, where the answer was then revealed. During the 1980s, in partnership with his art director Ron Brown, they were responsible for a D&AD award-winning Sainsbury's campaign. The advertisements were written and art-directed in a consciously stylish way, to reflect Sainsbury's aspirational brand values.

However, in the 1990s press and magazine advertising took on a new direction in an effort to break the stereotypical look of the advertisement. Creative teams begun to experiment with a more editorial style – the idea being that the reader might think it was part of the paper or magazine. This break with tradition meant that on many occasions the visual became much more important to the communication than the copy.

The big green triangle is back. Quality Street

Quality Street The big toffee finger has arrived.

Sainsbury's (opposite)

This stylish magazine campaign epitomised the craft of copywriting and art direction at its very best. Intriguing headlines lead into well-researched and beautifully written body copy. The art direction complemented the copy with stunning photography, adding an extra dimension to the communication.

Client: Sainsbury's / Agency: Abbott Mead Vickers BBDO Limited

The big green triangle. The big toffee finger. (this page)

Quality Street sweets are so big that their wrappers can stop trains! Using this surrealist imagery certainly delivers the unexpected to the viewer.

Client: Nestle Rowntree / Agency: Lowe London / Creative Director: Damon Collins / Art Director and Copywriter: Ed Morris / Photographer: David Stuart / Typographers: Ed Morris and Neil Craddock.
Image supplied courtesy of the D&AD Global Awards (Campaigns Consumer Magazines sponsored by The Evening Standard: Silver Nomination, 2004)

The visual

Contemporary creative advertising has largely abandoned long copy advertisements and many campaigns nowadays rely almost solely on the power of an imaginative and impactful visual to communicate the brand message. The 'media savvy' newspaper or magazine reader is well accustomed to images and accepts their instant communicative effect far more readily than that of long text. Within some campaigns it is hard to differentiate between the poster and press/magazine treatment if both use a strong visual concept, without having to adapt and change the concept dramatically for use across a range of media.

Tap (right)

This 2005 press ad for Honda still shows that well written copy and an intriguing visual work for brands that want to stand out from the crowd.

Client: Honda / Agency: Wieden + Kennedy London / Art Directors: Tony Davidson and Chris Groom / Copywriters: Simon MacTaggart and Nick Darken / Typographer: Chris Groom / Photographer: Guido Mocafico

Concept cars. Aren't they fantastic?
Cars that park themselves. Cars that hover.
But are they only exciting because they never get made?
What if one actually made it onto the production line?
Like the Honda FCX. A car that runs on hydrogen.
Whose only emission is pure water.
Maybe then we'd call them 'reality cars'.
Do you believe in the power of dreams?

Hippo (above)

This press ad features a photograph by Nick Georghiou, shot on an airfield in Norfolk, England (not Africa as you may have imagined!). A model of a hippo was used and later blended with the image of a real hippo.

Client: Landrover / Agency: Rainey Kelly Campbell Roalfe/Y&R / Creative Director: Mark Roalfe / Art Director: Jerry Hollens / Copywriter: Mike Boles / Photographer: Nick Georghiou

Different page sizes

Press advertising opportunities come in all shapes and sizes. Double page spreads (two facing pages), full, half or quarter page – in fact if you come up with an idea that benefits from an unusually shaped space, it may be possible! The example shown on this page (a student portfolio piece), demonstrates how effective the choice and position for your creative concept is, and in this case the whole concept revolves around the position of the advertisement on the family announcements page of a local newspaper. Magazines are even more flexible, with creative opportunities such as foldouts and gatefolds available to the advertiser.

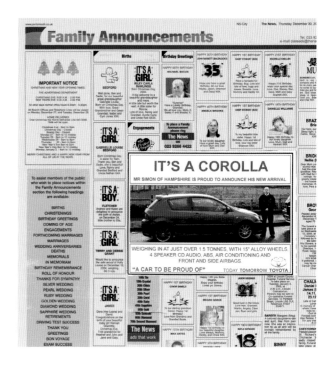

Cuba cigar (below)

This Virgin Atlantic ad ran across the bottom of newspaper pages.

Client: Virgin Atlantic / Agency: Rainey Kelly Campbell Roalfe/Y&R / Creative Director: Mark Roalfe / Art Director: Phil Kitching / Copywriter: Dean Iqbal / Photographer/illustrator: Alan Aldridge, plus 3D imaging from Actis / Typographer: Nils Leonard

It's a Corolla (above)

This student portfolio piece by David Rose demonstrates how effective the choice and positioning of your creative concept is. In this case the whole concept revolves around the position of the advertisement in the family announcements page of a local newspaper.

Concept and execution: David Rose

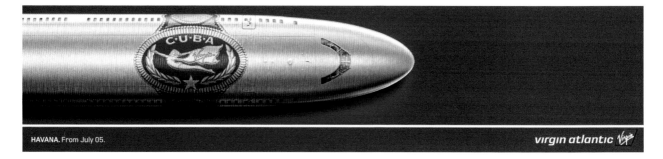

HAVANA. From July 05.

virgin atlantic

Advantages of the medium

- Newspapers communicate with different socio-economic groups, allowing the advertiser to reach these different groups effectively. The creative team can use a different language and tone of voice for specific interest groups.
- Magazine advertising also offers this advantage – with titles covering everything from football, rugby, computers and fashion to minority hobbies such as model and stamp-collecting, advertisers can reach different and disparate target groups.
- Magazines allow for more unusual formats such as fold outs and gatefolds. Free samples of products can also be attached to the page and brochures can be inserted into the magazine. In fact if you want a piece of direct mail to reach the target group, a magazine insert does the job (see Direct mail, p.58).
- National press provides the copywriter with the opportunity to craft long copy advertisements, so stories can be told.
- The frequency of newspapers and magazines offers the chance to be topical. Why not take an item of news and create an advertisement that links a brand directly to it?
- The agency can place advertisements in 'interest' sections within newspapers and magazines.
- Magazines use quality reproduction (the printing and paper quality is of a high standard). This allows the creative team to employ strong production values in the execution of the advertisement.

Disadvantages of the medium

- Printed media lacks the advantages of television advertising, such as movement and sound.
- Newspapers are full of clutter (other ads, editorial, stories and pictures), which hinders the communication process.
- Newspapers have a short life span – in other words they are read and then dumped (recycled hopefully!). Magazines stay around the house for a longer period – collected and filed away or given to your best friend to read. Some even end up in the doctor's waiting room.
- Newspapers generally suffer from poor reproduction, especially of colour. The use of spot colour (the use of a single colour, normally red, to highlight a starburst or a headline), can look 'cheap'.
- Colour pages are limited in some newspapers.

Do it!

Produce a series of advertisements for the fictitious flower company sayitwithflowers.com. Ensure you use the national press medium to its best advantage.

The purpose behind these ads is to create awareness of this new and exciting flower delivery dot-com. The service is based on the flowers arriving the next day anywhere within the country, along with a personalised message printed on a personally selected decorative card.

Your task is to find an interesting way to advertise this service in the national press – you will be judged by the response you get to the adverts (hits on the website). Think about the position and size of the space for the advert. Are there any special days it would be better to advertise on? If so, they may influence your ideas for the advertising concept.

TV and cinema

With the number of terrestrial stations increasing, as well as the expanding growth of satellite and digital channels, the advertiser has numerous opportunities to communicate with their increasingly fragmented audiences. Although television is not suitable for all advertisers (largely due to budget restrictions/expense as TV commercials are expensive to produce and air), many major brands use the medium regularly because of its powerful reach and ability to develop a strong brand image and awareness. The renewed popularity of the cinema as a leisure activity has also revived and fuelled the success of cinema advertising. The cinema allows brand messages to be communicated to a captive audience that is waiting to be entertained and willing to absorb the information presented to them on the big screen.

Fisherman and bear (above)

This humourous commercial features a 'brown bear' (actually an actor) who is extremely adept at fishing for salmon – so much so that a local fisherman attempts to steal the bear's catch. This results in a hilarious kung fu fight between the two. What better way to communicate the proposition that John West use only the best and freshest fish.

Client: John West / Agency: Leo Burnett / Creative Directors: Nick Bell and Mark Tutsell / Art Director: Paul Silburn / Agency Producer: Charlie Gatsky Production Company: Spectre / Production Company Director: Daniel Kleinman / Production Company Producer: David Botterrell / Editor: Steve Gandolphi at Cut & Run / Director of Photography: Steve Blackman

Balls (left)

This innovative commercial for Sony's Bravia televisions showered an entire block in San Francisco with coloured balls – a 'really simple celebration of colour'. No computer generated images were used in the production. The film was set to an acoustic soundtrack of Jose Gonzalez's 'Heartbeats'.

Client: Sony / Agency: Fallon London / Executive Creative Directors: Richard Flintham and Andy McLeod / Creative Director: Richard Flintham / Art Director/Copywriter: Juan Cabral / Director: Nicolai Fuglsig / Production company: MJZ

noitulovE (right)

The concept that good things are worth waiting for is taken to the ultimate extreme when two Guinness drinkers are transported back in time and are transformed to simple prehistoric creatures.

Client: Guinness / Agency: Abbot Mead Vickers BBDO Limited / Copywriter: Ian Heartfield / Art Director: Matt Doman / Production Company: Kleinman Productions / Director: Danniel Kleinman

The power of the commercial

The television and cinema commercial is still regarded by advertisers as the most powerful and persuasive medium. For most creative teams, working on television commercials may well be the highlight of their career. Unlike other more static media such as press and poster campaigns, television or cinema commercials offer the chance to tell a story, through a bespoke 30 or 40 second film about the brand or product. Using a combination of live action, special effects, dialogue, music and voice-overs provides the creative team with a chance to realise their concept in a powerful way through the development of a script and storyboard.

Only as recently as 50 years ago, commercials were very basic, almost live action 'press' advertisements. Many featured presenters talking directly to camera, giving testimonials and demonstrations of the product. It was only when the agency copywriters and art directors began to write scripts which used the medium to its full potential that specialist film companies began to take the genre seriously. For the creative team, television advertising had massive creative possibilities and media opportunities.

Cog (this page)

This captivating film breaks the mould of the typical car commercial. For nearly two minutes the viewer of Honda's Cog commercial is treated to a choreographed ballet of cogs turning, windscreen wipers crawling and various car bits playing their part in the event, when eventually the Honda Accord is revealed. The Heath Robinson associations are clear, however this film takes the concept into another dimension.

Client: Honda UK / Product: Accord / Agency: Wieden + Kennedy London / Creative team: Ben Walker and Matt Gooden / Creative Directors: Tony Davidson and Kim Papworth

The production process

This section will give a brief outline of the production process up to the shooting of a commercial, reviewing the relationship between the agency and the production company and the part each plays in the process. The focus here is on the creative, planning and production processes.

The agency producer

This role provides a link between the advertising agency and the production company. The agency producer liaises with the creative team and ensures that the director and the production company selected are best suited to the script. Arriving at this decision requires viewing different show reels and arranging preliminary meetings with shortlisted directors and production houses. These meetings are important for the creative team as they provide a chance to discover whether there is a 'shared vision' on how the storyboard should be shot and produced. Typically, the agency will get three companies to pitch and the best pitch wins. The agency producer is also responsible for overseeing and monitoring the budget.

The production company producer

The production company producer's main task is to project manage the commercial, organising locations, props, hiring the film crew and equipment and all contractual issues. He or she is responsible for the organisation of the shoot and all post-production issues including editing, special effects, music and voice-overs. Although large companies employ directors' representatives, whose job is to sell their directors' previous work to agency producers and creative teams, in smaller production houses this will be part of the producer's job. On many occasions the agency may have a specific director in mind, however sometimes there is a necessity to see up-and-coming directors whose work may not be as familiar to the agency team.

Animation

The use of animation in television and cinema commercials has always been popular with advertisers. The creation of brand characters such as Kellogg's Frosties' Tony the Tiger and in more recent years Bertie Bassett (Liquorice Allsorts) proved hugely successful for the products they promoted, creating affection and a long-term relationship with the consumer.

Animation allows the creative team to devise scripts that push the boundaries of their audience's imagination. It is a great medium for creating fantasy scenes or depicting fictitious characters or creatures, and can in some ways give you more creative freedom than live action. Animation is obviously a particularly good medium for advertising aimed at children.

Hand rendered or computer generated drawings are normally animated frame-by-frame. However, using stop-frame animation, characters or objects can be manipulated and brought to life. The feature film *Who Framed Roger Rabbit?* (1988) popularised the interplay of animated characters and live actors, and commercials were quick to use this technique. Other animation techniques include 'real time' animation, which uses puppeteers and their puppets to create the action. Even in live action commercials there are invariably some elements of graphic animation, whether it's a logo swivelling around or the campaign slogan appearing on the screen letter by letter.

We see one man talk to another. We hear a series of words about abuse that form a speech bubble coming out of his mouth. As he speaks more and more the bubble gets bigger and bigger. It then detaches from the man's mouth and floats away.

AS WE CUT AWAY FROM ONE SCENE AND DRIFT INTO THE NEXT IT IS AS IF OUR VIEW IS ATTACHED TO ONE OF THE SPEECH BUBBLES – FLOATING JUST ABOVE EACH SCENE.

We cut to see a mother park a car in a tight spot on a busy high street. She has a child in the back. We see the mother is looking very stressed. There's a parking warden walking up the street towards them, the mobile phone is going and her son is asking for something repeatedly. She turns around and reaches across the back of the seat before letting loose with her right hand – the child is stunned into silence…

MOTHER: DO YOU WANT ANOTHER ONE, DO YOU? WELL THEN SHUT UP, SHUT UP!

The mother gets out of the car and goes to the parking meter. Her back is turned to us as she scrapes through her purse for change. The speech bubble enters frame through the car window and engulfs the child.

WE CUT AWAY. OUR VIEW THEN DRIFTS INTO…

It's nighttime and we see a couple putting on their coats; they are dressed for a night out. They are talking loudly in front of a little girl who is sitting on the floor playing with a couple of buttons on the floor.

MOTHER: Don't worry about her, she can look after herself…

As the front door slams and adults voices drift off into the night.

MAN: You staying at mine tonight?

WOMAN: Yeah, why not?

To one side of frame the speech bubble appears and engulfs the little girl in peace and serenity.

WE CUT AWAY. OUR VIEW THEN DRIFTS INTO…

A little boy is sitting in the corner of a sofa. He is in a state of frozen alertness. His Dad sits next to him drinking a can of lager and smoking a cigarette. He shouts at the boy.

DAD:OI! Get me another can.

The boys eyes are wide open in total shock – the order he's been dreading has finally come but he's still frozen to the spot.

DAD: I SAID GET ME ANOTHER. YOU STUPID OR SOMETHING?

The Dad reaches across the sofa with his cigarette. Before any contact is made the son snaps out of it and walks towards the kitchen.

He opens the fridge, stands on his tiptoes and takes down a can of lager. As he turns around and starts to walk back towards the living room, one of the speech bubbles drops down in front of the little boy. He is so distracted he doesn't notice the bubble is there and walks straight into it. The bubble now protects him. The father walks out into the corridor. He starts to shout and scream at the boy.

DAD: YOU'RE TAKING YOUR TIME.

But now the boy is within the bubble and protected. The father's screams are muffled and vague.

WE CUT AWAY. OUR VIEW THEN DRIFTS INTO…

It is early one morning. We see a boy cowering in the corner of a bed, he is confused – there is emotional and physical hurt as well as the affection he still feels for his abuser. In the foreground, shrouded in darkness, a man wearing a dressing gown puts his finger to his lips. He then slips out of the room.

VO: JUST BY TALKING ABOUT IT, YOU CAN HELP PROTECT A CHILD FROM ABUSE…

Another speech bubble enters frame and floats over and around the child, engulfing him in warmth and security.

The speech bubble with the abused boy inside rises into the sky away from the abuse.

…DURING FULL STOP WEEK READ YOUR FULL STOP PACK AND FIND OUT THE OTHER WAYS YOU CAN ACT.

As it goes off into the distance it turns into the NSPCC Full Stop symbol.

SUPER: CRUELTY TO CHILDREN CAN STOP. FULL STOP.

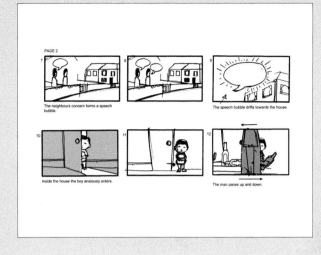

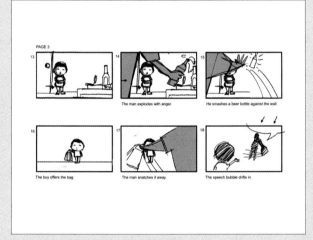

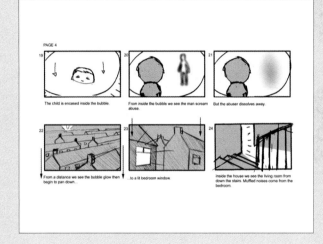

Talk 'til it stops

This script (opposite) and line-drawn storyboard (this page) present the idea that reporting cruelty to children can protect them from further harm in a clever way, easily understood by both children and adults. Speech bubbles literally surround and protect vulnerable children (see final execution overleaf).

Client: NSPCC / Creative agency: Saatchi & Saatchi / Copywriter: Joel Bradley / Art Director: Graham Lang / Production company: Nexus / Directors: Adam Foulkes and Alan Smith

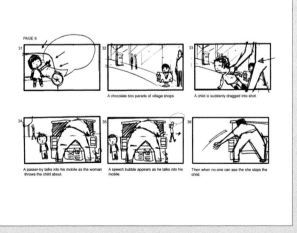

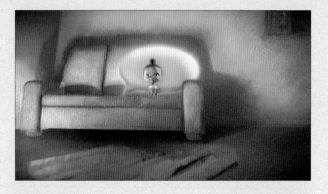

FULL STOP WEEK 3-10 OCT. READ YOUR MAIL PACK.

Talk 'til it stops. **FULL STOP** ● NSPCC

www.talktilitstops.com

Talk 'til it stops (this page)
Key frames from the final ad for NSPCC.

All credits listed on page 51

Advantages of the medium

- The television commercial has the power to create big brands with its mass coverage and impact created by action/movement, sound and colour.
- Anything is possible – don't be limited. If your script requires Martians eating instant mashed potato, then so be it.
- The length of the commercial offers a degree of flexibility. Commercials lasting 30, 40 or 60 seconds each offer different possibilities. There is also the opportunity to 'top and tail' the commercial break with short 'teaser' advertisements.
- The hundreds of channels on digital TV allow advertisers to reach fairly fragmented and specialist audiences.
- Using the right spots, advertisers can reach a vast audience with the brand's message or advertising concept. Television and cinema commercials have the power to interrupt people's lives.
- Commercials can show the product in action, thus demonstrating its effectiveness. Consider the case of car and tyre advertising, where manoeuvrability and road handling in the most difficult of weather conditions can be demonstrated.
- Television or cinema commercials can show 'real' people and portray 'a slice of life' that the target audience can relate to. Equally, the use of famous people or fictional characters has also been a rich source of inspiration for the advertising creative team and provided the opportunity for celebrity brand endorsement.
- Commercials can incorporate a musical jingle or catchphrase that can become part of everyday language for a short while. For example, in 1999 the American beer Budweiser commercials featured a 'whassup' catchphrase that was soon echoed in numerous bars.
- The use of a carefully chosen soundtrack to accompany the commercial can connect the target audience to the brand. It can even produce a chart hit for the artist (and the associated publicity spin-off for the brand), as Babylon Zoo's 'Spaceman' and Smoke City's 'Underwater Love' proved through their association with the Levi's brand.

Disadvantages of the medium

- Television is generally expensive to produce, and to buy the space (media). The logistics of making a commercial that features actors, set builds or a location shoot, special effects and editing involves many layers of expertise.
- The whole production process, from concept to screening, is relatively slow. The average live action commercial takes three months to produce.
- Viewers sometimes use the commercial break to do something else or surf other channels. So there is a chance many people will not see the commercial.
- There are tighter restrictions on television commercials, compared to press and magazine advertising, on what can and cannot be shown.
- If your story is complex, it can be difficult to convey the message or information in the allotted commercial time. If you are required to give the viewer detailed information, a short television or cinema commercial will not suffice.

Do it!

Devise a TV script for Guinness that uses the commercial break to its creative advantage. Your script can be as long or short as you want, or it can be separated into different sections. The commercial idea and use of the medium must be linked directly to the product.

Show your idea as a black and white storyboard (4–6 frames should be enough to get the idea across). Remember Guinness's brand image as a premium beer – sophisticated and cool!

Radio

The non-visual medium of radio might appear to limit creative scope and present several communication problems for advertisers. Some products and brands seem naturally to lend themselves towards visual media. However, the only real limitations are the bounds of your own imagination as a writer. Sometimes brands that seem least likely to adapt well to advertising on the radio can, with a little creative insight, use the medium in original and novel ways. The key to writing effective radio commercials is to first understand how, why and when radio audiences listen. After that, you can start to look at the different tools and techniques that can be used. Many of these are unique in the way that they are used in radio.

Creating memories radio script (below)
A tactical, price-led offer promoting day trips to the Isle of Wight.

Client: Red Funnel / Agency: Lawton / Copywriter: Tim John

Radio listening habits (below left)
By the 1930s, radio had reached most American homes, with families tuning in religiously to listen to their favourite programmes. This allowed advertisers to reach new audiences with their commercials.

Image reproduced courtesy of Retrofile/Getty images

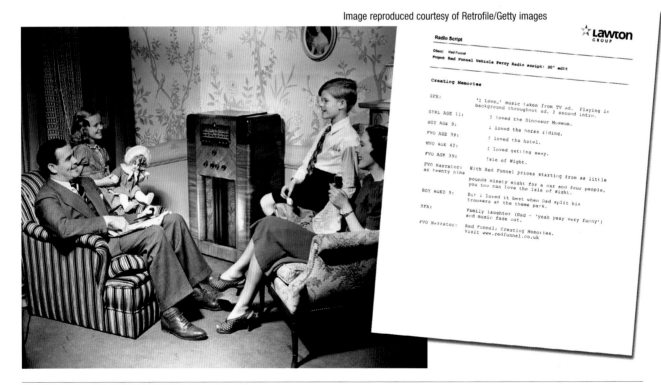

How listeners listen

Audiences listen to the radio in one of two ways: habitual or discretionary. 'Habitual' listening refers to routine patterns of listening behaviour: the listener can be expected to tune in to the same radio programmes with predictable frequency. Habitual listening tends to occur during peak hours, either early in the morning when the audience is getting ready for (or travelling to) work and during the working day itself.

'Discretionary' listening refers to the conscious and selective choice of channel or programme by a listener. As a result, audience attention and involvement levels are normally higher when the listening mode is discretionary. Discretionary listening generally occurs during leisure periods, when audiences can give more commitment to the radio programme they are listening to.

Why and when listeners listen

There are broadly two reasons why listeners listen to the radio: 'functional' or 'emotional'. Functional reasons include the need to check things like traffic reports or weather forecasts. Emotional reasons may be guided by the relationship that the listener may have with a particular programme or presenter, or the listener's preference for a particular genre of music.

In the morning, listeners' individual requirements can invariably shift between the functional and the emotional. Across many households at breakfast time, the radio is a shared experience, there in the background to wake people up and prepare them for work. Some people may be selectively listening for items of news and this may continue as a functional role of the radio as they travel into work with the radio on in their car.

During the day, the listening mode is dependent upon the environment. In the workplace, where it is a shared experience and the programme is chosen by consensus, the listening mode is habitual and the function of the radio is to provide the appropriate mood and atmosphere. In the home, the radio is often switched on to provide 'company' while undertaking the daily tasks. In this environment, programme choice tends to be more personal and selective, even though the attention and involvement of the listener may be low.

In the evening or at weekends, listeners' attention and involvement is normally much higher as there is a stronger degree of personal involvement and recreational choice.

Use the fact that your listeners can't see!

The fact the creative team has no visuals or moving images to illustrate its radio advertisement need not lessen the impact of their message. When used effectively, radio commercials can exploit the fact that the audience has nothing to see to maximise the surprise and subsequent impact of the message in a unique and compelling way.

With radio advertising, the images normally found in print campaigns or television and cinema commercials are instead formed in the mind of the listener. The words, phrases and tone of the radio script will trigger certain associations and references in the listener's mind, which will allow him or her to visualise those images in a directly personal and relevant way. One of the key skills in writing for radio is to know your audience well enough to know what you need to say or suggest in order to plant the right kind of images in their mind's eye, just enough to allow their imagination to take over.

Set the scene

It is important to load the opening lines of your script with enough information to provide the listener with a reference point from which they can visualise what is going on. If your script includes characters, then the listener will need to know who they are, where they are, and what they are doing. Sometimes you can do this very simply with some well considered opening lines and sound effects. One character can refer to the other as a friend, colleague or family member. He or she can make comments or observations that provide clues about the setting and environment your characters inhabit.

By allowing one character to refer to other people in the scene, the mind of the listener can be led to visualise a cast of more than just the one or two characters that speak the lines of your script. The ambient sounds of a crowded public place can help to reinforce this illusion. Think of where your scene is set – is it inside or outside? If it is inside, is it in a large hall or a small, confined room? If it is outside, is it hot or cold, wet, dry or windy? Why are your characters there in the first place? Think of what you need to do to provide the listener with the answers to these questions, quickly and simply.

The 'reveal'

As radio listeners can't 'see' an advertisement, the creative team has a greater opportunity to confound their expectations with cleverly written dialogue and sound effects that keep the audience guessing (or mis-guessing) right up to the final twist of the script. The skill is to get the listener to think that something is going to happen (or has happened) and then to do something completely different. The 'reveal' is a term used to define that moment in the script when the significance of the scene and the advertising message or proposition is crystal clear. When the reveal is unexpected and takes the listener by surprise, the moment can have the same strength of impact as the punchline of a joke. When it is allied to the advertising message in this way, the reveal can be extremely effective.

Give your characters definition

The way an advertisement's characters speak to each other can provide the listener with a lot of information and can also help make the characters more believable. Endowing characters with status affects the way they talk, the words they choose to use, the things they choose to say or not say. It affects whether they lead or dominate the conversation, whether they interrupt or wait to be invited to speak. By creating an imbalance of status between characters, they become more clearly defined and sound more convincing.

Similarly, allowing characters to express emotions raises questions in the mind of the listener and makes the characters and the story more compelling. If one of the characters is introduced at the beginning of the commercial expressing anger, sadness or some other extreme emotion, the story immediately becomes more interesting. If they are sobbing uncontrollably or laughing hysterically, we automatically want to know why.

Adding detail can also increase character definition. This need not involve extending the script by many words – it is a case of being selective in the choice of elements you use to reflect the nature of you character, to enhance the image in the mind of the listener.

However, the key to creating interesting and believable characters in a radio commercial is for the writer to know their characters well. Perhaps by visualising someone they know who fits the profile of their character and then developing the character's persona.

Write the 'pre-scene'

When creating characters for a radio commercial, it is also important to establish their relationship to other characters in the script. This can be achieved by creating a 'pre-scene'. The pre-scene is the sequence of events leading up to the scene captured in the commercial. The pre-scene can be developed by identifying and then answering all of the questions that could possibly be asked of the commercial's characters and scenario. Writing the pre-scene enables the creative team to understand their characters in more depth. By giving the characters a reason for their behaviour and reactions, the pre-scene helps to develop a greater sense of realism and believability.

Sound effects

Sound effects (SFX), together with music, can be useful tools for evoking a mood or establishing a location in a radio commercial. However, they need to be used cautiously – there is a danger that without the support of images, the sound effects may be ambiguous or unsuitable. In a television commercial, the sight of bacon frying in a pan, accompanied by the sound of it sizzling, is so powerful that the viewer can practically smell it. In radio however, there is a real danger that the sound of bacon sizzling might be mistaken for the sound of water being poured (often used as a sound effect in tea and coffee advertisements) and is easily confused with the sound of someone urinating!

Advantages of the medium

- Radio campaigns can be run regionally or nationally. The capacity to run campaigns on local radio stations can enable better targeting of an audience by location.
- Compared to television, radio campaigns are relatively cheap in terms of airtime and production.
- Budgets can stretch further, allowing commercials to be played more frequently and for longer periods of time to build coverage and awareness.
- Airtime can be bought to target different listeners at different times of the day such as 'drivetime', reaching business people travelling to and from work.
- People can listen to radio in circumstances where watching a television or reading a magazine would be impossible.
- Radio tends to be a more intimate and conversational medium that allows listeners to conjure up their own mental images.

Disadvantages of the medium

- With the exception of breakfast shows, individual radio stations' listening figures are relatively low compared to other media audiences (e.g. TV).
- There is a danger that people will get tired of hearing the same commercial over and over again. Some commercials can be particularly annoying when heard several times a day.
- The multitude of commercial radio stations crowding the airwaves can dilute each station's share of the market.
- The lack of any visual image means that the commercial has to work harder to match the dramatic impact of television.

Do it!

The ability to create a story and develop characters is at the heart of writing radio commercials. These exercises are provided courtesy of Mandy Wheeler, Creative Director of Punch It Up.

1. Concentrate on one aspect of your character. Write about some specific detail, e.g. what is under their bed, in their kitchen cupboard, in their medicine cabinet, in their toolbox? Make this important to the character and revealing about their personality.

2. Write a story or a piece of dialogue in which the character expresses a viewpoint or belief about life. Choose a viewpoint that is very different from your own. Make sure that the attitude is revealed in what the character does as well as what they say (i.e. 'show' as well as 'tell').

3. Create a character using the method above, but stop when you get the basic outline of name, age, job etc. Create a list of all the stereotypical characteristics of that kind of person/job. Now continue to create the character without using any of those characteristics.

Direct mail

fit a particular profile, but who don't have any previous or current relationship with the brand or product.

In a recent survey, people were asked what they did with the last piece of direct mail they received, only 40% actually opened and read it, 40% put it straight in the bin and the remaining 20% were opened, but the contents weren't interesting enough to warrant any further attention (*Consumer Direct Mail Trends Survey*, 2004).

So if there is such a high degree of negativity about direct mail, why do advertisers do it? The answer is because it is has been proven to be effective. While it's almost impossible to establish the impact a cinema commercial has on a target market, direct mail allows you to ascertain exactly how many people responded to each mailing, and of those how many converted to sales. Through direct mail, clients can establish a dialogue with their customers and this can have a positive impact on the brand as well as increase sales.

Many consumers view direct mail (solicited or unsolicited literature mailed to existing or prospective customers) as unwanted 'junk' mail, and many in the advertising industry also share this view. Historically, direct mail campaigns were seen as a second-class medium, both creatively and in terms of recipient appeal. However, even the most hardened advertising aficionados can see the benefits of a well-planned, creative direct mail campaign; direct mail can be tailored to a particular audience demographic and even speak on a one-to-one basis with a named individual. In reality though, not all direct mail is perfectly targeted, highly personalised and encased in creative mailing packs that are gratefully received.

Direct mail is personalised with an individual's name and address, but door drop mailshots (unsolicited, non-personalised literature delivered to prospective customers' homes) are not. Receiving a door drop mailshot doesn't mean that it hasn't been targeted in some way (such as location or spending patterns), but it does mean that the sender does not possess your personal details on their database.

Direct mail will generate a better response if the individuals targeted are existing customers or have previously requested information about the brand/product at some point. However, mailing databases often contain lists of 'cold' individuals who

Pasta mailer (above)
The Guardian sent out their message on a piece of lasagne to promote the serialisation of a recipe book in their magazine supplement.

Client: *The Guardian* / Agency: Claydon Heeley / Creative Directors: Dave Woods and Pete Harle / Art Directors: Simon Haslehurst and Gary Fraser / Copywriter: Kristian Wheater

Client databases

Client databases are vital to a successful direct mail campaign for many reasons. At the simplest level, databases keep records of an organisation's customers, with the name and address details of potential mail recipients. The database can then be updated with the details of any mailshots that have been sent out and whether they generated a response. Records of 'goneaways' should also be deleted from the database to keep it 'live', i.e. up to date. Goneaways are the names of people who no longer live at that address – that's why direct mail packs always include a return address on the back of the envelope.

Enhanced databases keep transaction data of an organisation's customers – information that can then be used to personalise the advertising message. Supermarket loyalty cards are a perfect example of this, and supermarkets use loyalty card information to send out thousands of different messages to their customers, each tailored specifically to individual consumer purchase profiles.

Databases also allow organisations to test different creative treatments and promotions to see which one is the most effective. So companies may test a mailing with a statement on the envelope, and compare it to a mailing without a similar statement to see which got a higher response. Direct mail agencies work with their clients to constantly refine their approaches, always seeking a combination that will yield even better results than previous mailings. Databases can be used not only to track response, but to build response and conversion models, i.e. an estimate of how many responses will convert to sales – so for every 100 people who request a brochure, how many will then go on to purchase the product or service?). This information can be used in campaign planning.

Tesco mailing (right)

Tesco uses the data generated by their loyalty card to produce highly targeted mailings to their customers. They know what their customers buy, so they can make sure that the offers they send out are relevant – if you regularly buy cat food, you won't receive offers for Pedigree Chum.

Client: Tesco / Agency: EHS Brann / Executive Creative Director: Patrick Baglee / Art Director: Libby Clay / Copywriter: Rachel Heathfield / Client Partner: Anna Dobson

Customer profiling

Organisations with customer databases can also profile their existing customers and use that knowledge to help them find more people with the same profile who could potentially become new customers. Sophisticated profiling systems such as ACORN and Mosaic can be used to profile customers by post/zip code so companies can pinpoint not only the areas that their customers come from, but by definition what kind of consumers they are likely to be (see Market research, p.76). This knowledge can then be used to buy listings of individuals with similar profiles to those identified on the database.

Mailing packs

Mailing packs are becoming more and more creative. As with all forms of advertising there is a need for direct mail to attract the target audience's attention. Potential customers are more likely to notice mailing packs that are different, or that include anything useful or interactive. However, you do have to be careful to make the creativity relevant and to avoid gimmicks, especially with existing customers who just want you to get to the point.

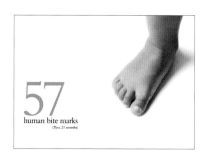

NSPCC mailshot (above)

This 'cold' direct mail pack (sent to new potential donors), was aimed at encouraging them to donate £2 (approx. US$3.70) a month. The visuals and copy were based on how trifling £2 (approx. US$3.70) is compared to the numerous injuries suffered by children.

Client: NSPCC / Agency: Rapp Collins / Art Director: Chris Spore / Copywriter: Nick Cooper

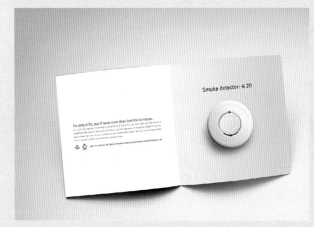

Smoke detector (above)

This powerful mailing pack vividly shows the devastation caused by fire. It has been designed to look like an upmarket furniture catalogue – the implication being that you spend all this money on furniture, but you can't be bothered to buy a smoke alarm.

Client: Brussels. Hoofdstedeijk, Gewest / Agency: TBWA/Brussels / Creative Director: Jan Dejonghe / Copywriter: Peter Slabbynck / Art Director: Alex Ameye / Photographer: Philippe Boels

Don't forget the 'PS'

Most mail packs include a brochure or leaflet and a letter containing lots of headlines and PSs to get the message across even if the recipient doesn't read the whole letter or brochure. A reply device in the form of a coupon, web address or telephone number is also essential. The great thing about direct mail is that there is plenty of space to say what you want to say. This makes it an ideal medium for any brand that needs to get a lot of information across – such as financial products, charities or holidays. It's also invaluable as a sales tool, which is why mail order companies send more mailings than any other industry.

Direct mail and IMC

There's no doubt that direct mail has gained credibility through Integrated Marketing Communications (IMC). Advertisers have been able to see how powerful their campaigns can be if they plan campaigns that run across different media, are timed to make the maximum impact and that talk with one voice. How much more effective will a campaign be if you see a powerful advertisement on TV, then a poster that shows just an element of that message, which prompts you to contact an organisation – and as a result of that contact you receive an effective and targeted mail pack? Ultimately this forms a very powerful message, carried across a range of media.

Stick with it (right)

The British Heart Foundation co-ordinated a brilliant campaign across a range of media to highlight the effects of smoking. They launched a powerful TV ad, graphically showing the effects of smoking on your arteries. This was supported by a poster campaign simply showing a cross-section of a cigarette filled with the fatty deposits that build up in smokers' veins. Anyone who called to ask for advice was then sent a mailing pack that was difficult to open because it contained a thick, gluey substance that really brought the message home.

Client: British Heart Foundation / Agency: EHS Brann / Executive Creative Director: Lu Dixon / Art Director: Adrian Richards / Copywriter: Russell Garn

Advantages of the medium

- Not only can mail be personalised by name, the message and any offers can also be tailored specifically to the customers – this makes it more personal than most other media.
- Direct mail can be measured in terms of response and conversion to sales. This is an advantage over other media, where it's often impossible to directly relate the campaign to sales.
- Direct mail can be used to establish a dialogue with customers, which makes it a potentially interactive medium.
- Once you've established a dialogue you can start to build a relationship with the customer. Charities are very good at doing this with their donors, with long-term communication programmes designed to build trust and loyalty.
- Direct mail can be used to sell directly to customers, thus avoiding the need to use retailers or intermediaries. This means that customers get better value because they don't have to pay a marked up price to cover commission or retail profit. The travel industry now use direct mail extensively as it avoids having to pay 10% commission to travel agents and it means they don't depend on travel agents choosing to sell them in over their competitors.
- Direct mail is a very useful way of getting across a message when there is a great deal that needs to be said. This can often be used to support a broadcast campaign.

Disadvantages of the medium

- Many see all direct mail as 'junk mail', so often important and relevant mailings get out in the bin before they are even opened.
- There is a great deal of wastage as response rates are relatively low. A company may be happy with a 10% response, but that does mean that 90% has potentially gone in the bin. That means that a large part of the direct mail budget has been wasted – this is why so much effort is put into finding ways to increase response rates.
- It is difficult to measure the effects of a direct mail campaign on brand awareness and attitude. The recipient may have opened and read a mailing, but not acted upon it at that time. The communication may have influenced what they think about the brand – either positively or negatively.
- Problems with delivery and fulfilment can often result in very negative experiences for customers – companies who sell through direct mail have to be very sure that they have got the right systems in place to fulfil orders on time.

Do it!

Collect two or three different direct mail packs and compare them. What similarities do you notice? Consider the elements of the pack such as the envelope, the letter, the leaflet and the reply device, as well as the tone of voice.

How do you think they got your details? Are you one of their customers or do you think they bought your name from a cold list?

What do you think each pack was trying to achieve? Was it simply selling something, or did it have other objectives such as building a relationship with you by rewarding your loyalty, or asking you to donate regularly to a charity? Was it really junk mail or actually something quite interesting when you looked at it in more detail?

Online advertising

The development of powerful computers and the increased use of broadband have enabled the rapid exchange of data and information. One sixth of the world's population has access to the internet, so it was inevitable that advertising agencies would discover the potential of online advertising to promote their client's brands and products. Online advertising is gathering pace and it is only a matter of time before more of the top creative talents are attracted to work in this exciting and relatively new sector of the industry.

A new creative opportunity

Online advertising has become a vital part of an integrated marketing communications programme, running alongside and complementing more traditional media. When used as a direct marketing tool, online advertising banner and pop-up advertisements work effectively for certain brands and products. Over the last few years banner adverts have become more sophisticated and creative, using live action film and animation to help interaction with the viewer. It also allows small companies in niche markets to advertise quickly and cheaply. However, these advertisements have a short 'shelf life' and need changing every week or two.

Part of online advertising's potential as a creative opportunity, is its newness. It is an experimental and constantly evolving medium, which means almost anything is possible for the advertising creative. Its newness also means that there are no mentors or models to follow or copy, allowing for original and fresh interpretations to be used. The internet as a medium is full of clutter, so it is crucial to be more creative than the next advertisement.

The medium's great advantage is its interactivity with the viewer – an instant two-way communication, whether they want it or not! Becoming a computer 'geek' is not compulsory, although an understanding of the medium and the capability of using software such as Image Ready, Fireworks and Flash to create the graphics and animation is advantageous.

Viral

'Viral marketing describes any strategy that encourages individuals to pass on a marketing message to others, creating the potential for exponential growth in the message's exposure and influence.' Ralph F. Wilson, Email Marketing and Online Marketing Editor, *Web Marketing Today*.

We have all received bad jokes and small films via email – we welcome some and forward them to our friends or colleagues, others we delete. Viral advertising works the same way, relying on the recipient interacting with communication in an email or through a website ad and sending it on. It is a 'word of mouth' process that soon results in the rapid spread of the communication. Sometimes viral websites are set up, featuring promotional games, contests and films that are hopefully sent on to friends. One of the earliest examples of viral marketing was the publicity campaign for the film *The Blair Witch Project*. An internet and viral campaign propagated rumours that the events in the film were real.

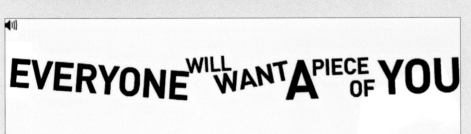

Starzine (this page)

Starzine is an online 'magazine' that is created by visitors to the MTV website. It enables users to upload images from their mobile phones and use graphic tools to create as many of their own pages as they wish. *Starzine* is also a competition; the pages voted most popular move towards the front of the magazine and the winning page becomes the front cover.

Glue created both the site and the ads that drove traffic to it. The ads ran across a range of MTV sites all over Europe, employing a deliberately bold and eye-catching illustrative style and some nice interactive touches to entice people in. The message was that 'everyone will want a piece of you'. Each execution showed a different result of fame.

Client: MTV / Agency: Glue London / Creative Director: Seb Royce / Creative Team: Christine Turner and Simon Lloyd / Designer: Dom O'Brien

Littler Britain (above)

This campaign was aimed at getting people out of their cars and back on to trains. Virgin tackled the widely held perception that trains were slow by comparison. The message was that as the new trains were faster than ever before, the UK felt even smaller than normal. A set of six films were seeded across various viral sites, and each film was given a different release date to keep it topical. Their first film, *Cockerel*, was released on the same day as the British *King Kong* premier. *Christmas* was released in December, and *Sick* was released just before the New Year.

Client: Virgin Trains / Agency: Glue London / Creative Director: Seb Royce / Creative Team: Christine Turner and Simon Lloyd / Designer: Adam Lee and Tomboy Virals

- Online advertising can be interactive, involving and engaging with your audience in a much more direct way than most advertising media.
- It is an ideal way of targeting a relatively young, technologically literate audience.
- Online advertising is viewable 24 hours a day.
- The internet can be quite anarchic/irreverent, allowing you to get away with more things than other media allow.
- Popular online ad campaigns can spread incredibly quickly and widely through viewers passing links/files on to friends – the so-called viral effect.
- Animation or films can easily be incorporated into online campaigns, giving you creative flexibility.

Disadvantages of the medium

- Online advertising is still very new, and has not yet been fully explored.
- It is restricted to people with access to computers – for instance you may find it difficult to target older people through online advertising.
- Individuals' screen preferences and low screen resolution can be challenging for the design and typography of online campaigns.

Do it!

Produce online advertising concepts to promote SAGA holidays to the over fifties.

First, thoroughly research this well-established holiday company and you will be amazed how this helps your initial ideas. Is it a good idea to use online advertising? It is certainly not the most obvious way to reach this target group – or is it? Many of this affluent group use the internet on a regular basis and are very computer literate. They have money to spend after downsizing their houses after their children have 'left the nest'. Maybe online advertising could be just one part of an integrated advertising campaign. See if online advertising can fit into the mix!

Natural Noodling (opposite)

To communicate the overwhelming 'irresistibly trashy' appeal of Pot Noodle, Glue focused on a viral game for the online campaign. Taking inspiration from topical stories in the tabloid press, Glue came across the phenomenon of 'dogging' – where couples travel to beauty spots in their cars to either watch or engage in 'coupling' with strangers. Replacing these illicit 'dogging' activities with 'Pot Noodle' represented 'irresistibly trashy' behaviour in a comical and subversive way; in the game people crave the snack so much that they're driven to 'noodling' in more and more inappropriate places - outdoors, with strangers etc. The game was developed as an interactive video piece set in a car park, with players having to establish which cars have 'noodlers' inside. The aim was to find as many people to noodle with as possible, before your Pot Noodle goes cold! The 'send to a friend' function increased the viral effect and ensured new visitors were constantly brought to the website.

Client: Pot Noodle / Agency: Glue London / Creative Director: Seb Royce / Creative Team: Gemma Butler and Gavin Rogers / Designer: Simon Cam

CHAPTER 2

CAMPAIGN PLANNING AND STRATEGY

The client

Most advertising campaigns are created by an agency, working on behalf of an organisation, corporation, manufacturer or individual; in all cases the 'client'. Few clients choose to handle their advertising internally, or 'in-house', as most appreciate that commissioning an agency can bring fresh ideas and objectivity to the job in hand.

In many ways the relationship between the client and the agency is mutually beneficial, but ultimately it is the client that controls the budget and can elect to move their account at any time. The agency's fear that an account might be moved can lead to their agreeing to a campaign strategy that they may not be entirely happy with, simply to accommodate the client's wishes. In such cases the results are often disastrous and the relationship between both parties can be irreparably damaged, as both parties blame each other for the failure of the campaign. The 'fear factor' still exists, but these days the relationship between the agency and the client tends to be built on a greater sense of partnership. Most major clients have learned to trust the judgement of their agencies and agencies have learned to involve the client in key stages of the process.

The client brief

Once the relationship between the client and agency is established, work on a campaign can begin. Every project starts with a brief from the client. This brief is usually in the form of a written document, which is then presented verbally to the agency. The client brief should clearly state the objectives of the campaign, based on a thorough analysis of the current status of the brand and its marketplace. The client brief shouldn't tell the agency how to do their job, but it should give them as much guidance and information as possible to help them arrive at the best solution.

Structuring the client brief

The British Institute of Practitioners in Advertising recently put together a best practice guide on behalf of a number of industry bodies (*The Client Brief*, 2003, IPA, London. Copies are available from www.ipa.org.uk). The guide includes a comprehensive list of what should be included in a client brief and communicated to an agency.

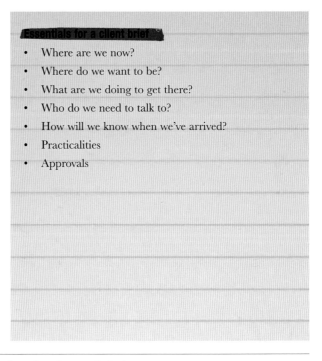

Essentials for a client brief

- Where are we now?
- Where do we want to be?
- What are we doing to get there?
- Who do we need to talk to?
- How will we know when we've arrived?
- Practicalities
- Approvals

Where are we now?

Firstly the client brief should detail the current position of the brand, product or service in terms of sales, market share, distribution, and consumer attitudes. The client must be completely honest about the brand/product/service and present its weaknesses as well as its strengths. It is also important for the brief to recognise any threats posed by competitors as well as any opportunities that are yet to be exploited.

A SWOT (Strengths, Weaknesses, Opportunities and Threats) analysis is a useful tool that allows the client to display the brand in the context of the marketplace which it operates in – see the example shown below.

Strengths

Examples of the brand's strong points in the marketplace. These are often compared to competitors, e.g. market leader.

Weaknesses

Any problems that the brand is facing. Might include issues such as consumers no longer finding the brand relevant or the fact that the product doesn't offer the same benefits as its competitors.

Opportunities

These might include the opportunity to market the brand to a new target audience or a change in legislation such as the inclusion of new member states into the EU.

Threats

The threat may come from a new competitor entering the marketplace or a change in legislation that may limit the marketing opportunities of the brand, e.g. potential restrictions on advertising to children and health issues such as Bird Flu.

Where do we want to be?

This next section of the brief should clarify the objectives of the campaign. What does the client see as the primary objective of the campaign; an increase in sales, or perhaps a shift in consumer perception of the brand? Knowing exactly what the client wants to achieve will help the agency to create a more targeted campaign.

What are we doing to get there?

The brief should include details of any and all other initiatives being undertaken at the same time by the client's marketing department to achieve those objectives. This will ensure that any new campaign created by the agency can be fully integrated into other marketing activities.

Who do we need to talk to?

This element of the client brief will perhaps be the most influential on the direction of the creative strategy and the media chosen to communicate the message. The client needs to tell the agency as much as possible about the target audience and potential customers; from who they are, to why they buy, might buy or currently don't buy the brand or product.

How will we know when we've arrived?

The client brief also needs to outline the criteria that will be used to evaluate the results of the campaign. This will usually involve some degree of market research both before and after the campaign.

Evaluation criteria are not always linked to sales, as advertising is just one part of the process that will encourage a consumer to purchase a product or service. Unless the campaign is one of direct response (for example, selling direct from the page or screen), then judging campaign success by sales numbers ignores the role that advertising plays in building consumer relationships and fostering brand loyalty.

Practicalities and approvals

Finally, the client brief should include all the details that relate to the project management of the campaign. What timescales are required, what's the budget and who is responsible for signing off the creative and media spend? If there are any constraints on media, or legal requirements that the agency should know about, then these should be covered in the brief.

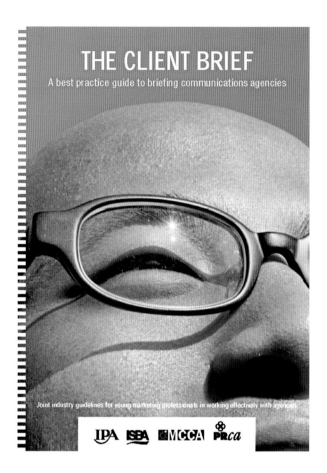

Industry Best Practice Guide (above and opposite)
Key industry trade bodies have created a number of Best Practice Guides, based on extensive industry research, which can be downloaded from www.ipa.co.uk

Extract from *The Client Brief*, a joint industry guide published July 2003 by the Institute of Practitioners in Advertising (IPA), the Incorporated Society of British Advertisers (ISBA), the Marketing Communication Consultants Association (MCCA) and the Public Relations Consultants Association (PRCA).

Garbage in, garbage out

Most agencies subscribe to the old adage of 'garbage in, garbage out'. If the client doesn't supply all the right information then how can the agency hope to come up with the right campaign strategy? This is where the value of the partnership between the client and the agency cannot be underestimated. If a client and agency are used to working with one another, then the agency will already know much of the information that would normally be included in the client brief. This inevitably saves time when it comes to briefing and minimises the risk of the agency coming up with inappropriate strategies.

FOREWORD

"FORGET, JUST FOR A MINUTE, THAT YOU ARE BRIEFING AN AGENCY. INSTEAD, PRETEND YOU ARE STANDING ON THE BANK OF A RIVER ABOUT TO BUILD A BRIDGE."

CHRIS HERD
IPA Value of Advertising Committee

Around you are architects, builders, all sorts of different experts that you have hired to help you. They might all come from different specialist companies, they might all come from a single one-stop-bridge-shop. It really doesn't matter. All that matters is that you build the best and most effective bridge you can.

So what brief should you give them in order to get that perfect bridge?

How about **where it should start from?**
Where are you standing right now? Where is 'point A'? They need to know that. That's not up for debate.

And what about **where it should finish?**
Where's 'point B'? The destination. If I were the architect, that's the bit of information I'd want made pretty clear.

Finally, what about **how to build the bridge itself?**

Probably not.

Maybe you'd give them some ideas on what the bridge might look like, what vehicles will need to cross it, what size boats will need to go underneath it, how high the hand-rails should be, etc, etc. But you're not going to tell them how to build the bridge. That's their job. You're going to sit back and wait to see the drawings.

It's the same with briefing agencies. They need to know where you are now. And they need to know where you want to get to. What will success look like? And how will it be measured?

If every agency involved in your campaign shares that same information, aren't they likely to work better together to achieve the desired result?

So when you're writing an agency brief, think "**Where am I now?**" and "**Where do I need to get to?**". Make it crystal clear. And you'll find that most agencies will be pretty good at getting you there.

I think that's the single biggest thing we've learned from all of our research in preparing this guide. So I hope it sings out loud and clear as our single biggest recommendation.

Now, back to bridges.

The Millennium footbridge. Wouldn't you just love to see the original client brief?

Do it!

Consider a current campaign of your choice. Try and write the client brief for this campaign.

What is the background to the campaign? What do you think the objectives of the campaign are? Who is the target audience and what does the client want them to think, feel or do as a result of the campaign?

How do you think they will evaluate the success of the campaign – through marketing research or by analysing sales?

What else does the agency need to know?

Although the client brief should include much of the information required by the agency to begin work on their campaign concept, it will invariably need to be supplemented. The client brief will define the brand's target audience, but it may not provide as much detail as the agency needs in order to ensure they create the right message.

The agency's account planning team is responsible for getting under the skin of the target audience, to empathise with them to such a degree that they begin to think as the customer thinks. The account planning team needs to discover what the target audience's attitudes are towards the product category, the buying process and the brand. This information will be vital to the development of an effective advertising strategy.

Attitudes to the product category

The target audience's attitude to the category within which the client's product or service sits will be vital to the direction of the campaign. A consumer is likely to take different considerations into account when buying a bar of chocolate, compared to buying a car or selecting a mortgage. Consumer attitudes will vary depending on whether the purchase requires them to commit to a lower or higher level of involvement.

Happiness (above)
Buying a bar of chocolate is a routine response requiring little thought from the consumer, compared to expensive decisions like buying a new car, which require a great deal of consideration.

Client: Cadbury Schweppes / Agency: Publicis UK / Art Director: Cat Silliman / Copywriter: Stephen Beverly / Creative Director: Nik Studzinski

Attitudes to the buying process

The account planning team must identify the processes involved in purchasing the product or service. Is it simply a routine response that requires little thought from the consumer, a limited response that takes a little more thought or an extensive decision that will require a great deal of consideration?

Investigating the buying process in detail allows account planners to gain a better understanding of what motivates the consumer. Do consumers feel positive or negative about the purchase? Is it a pleasant experience or a chore? If the purchase does require some thought, where do consumers go for information or advice about which product to buy? This knowledge will help planners to define the advertising strategy and will inform the media planning process.

There is no exact model for understanding purchase behaviour in terms of why consumers may choose to buy a particular product, as attitudes will vary between different target audiences, but purchase price and consumer income are of course key factors.

Attitudes to the brand

As well as the product category and the buying process, the account planning team must finally explore the target audience's attitude to the brand. This will help create a picture of where the brand is positioned in relation to its competitors, and will help define ways in which the brand can be differentiated from similar products or services. For example, do consumers view the brand as a quality or value product? Do they see the brand as a friend or a functional product that is best at doing what needs to be done? Do they only buy your brand or do they sometimes buy others – and if so why? When do they use the brand – frequently or seldom, every day or only on special occasions?

Often the objective of the campaign will be to change or shift some of these attitudes so the consumer views the brand, the purchase and the use of the product or service in a different light.

Do it!

You are the account planner working on a new Mediterranean cruise product aimed at the grey market (adults aged 55+). You need to start thinking like someone who is 30 years older than you. Put yourself in their shoes and try to imagine the stages that you might go through when booking a cruise – then analyse how this differs from when you last booked a holiday.

Market research

Market research underpins virtually all of the decisions made at the campaign planning stage. Through market research both the client and the agency are better able to understand the marketplace, identify and profile the target audience, test their creative ideas, choose the most appropriate media form and, finally, evaluate the success of the campaign.

The client will normally provide basic and initial research about the target market and audience in the client brief, which is then supplemented by research undertaken by the agency.

Omnibus surveys

Market research is a vast area, underpinned by a variety of different methodologies. Many clients commission their own market research to investigate those issues that are directly relevant to their brand, but organisations may also buy into external research sources.

An omnibus survey is undertaken by a dedicated market research company and conducted on a regular basis. Organisations can then pay to have a specified number of questions included in the survey. These surveys are particularly useful for tracking changes in brand consumption and awareness before and after an advertising campaign.

Agencies may also buy data from different sources to assist them with their planning. This is usually supplied by syndicated data services; companies that collect general information and sell it to clients. Mintel and Keynote are two examples of this, operating in numerous countries. Both produce detailed market reports using information compiled from many different sources. These market reports are very useful in helping to track competitive activity and to understand issues relating to a market as a whole. They also consider future trends, which companies can then match to their own predictions.

Research methods

Market research companies are best placed to advise on the most appropriate methods for a specific purpose. Their choice and selection of research techniques will be influenced by three key factors: what the client wants to establish, how many individuals will need to be canvassed and what the budget for market research is.

Primary research is information gained directly from the consumer, either by a survey or by observation. The client or agency will usually employ specialist market research to generate primary research data.

Secondary research is generated from information that already exists. This could be as simple as looking at sales data and analysing trends, or it could be more sophisticated market reports based on a variety of internal and external sources.

Qualitative research focuses on extracting in-depth information from the target market, which helps agencies and clients to develop a better understanding of what the consumer thinks or feels about a topic, and why. So if you want to know how they feel about buying a particular product, what they think about colours used in the packaging or what the brand really means to them, then you are much more likely to conduct focus group sessions (see below). Generalisations cannot be drawn from this sort of research, but this approach does help to build a deeper understanding of the consumer.

Quantitative research requires significantly more responses and is focused on fact. The information obtained tends to provide clearer and more quantifiable answers, which are less prone to subjective interpretation. So if you want to track someone's purchase patterns for a particular product you may use a questionnaire to ask when they buy the product, how often and where. Questionnaires are the most commonly used method to acquire quantitative data, as these can be conducted by mail, telephone or on the Internet.

Survey methods

- Mail surveys: questionnaires delivered through the post.
- Consumer purchase diaries: consumers are asked to keep shopping diaries.
- Telephone surveys: questionnaires or in-depth interviews conducted by telephone.
- Street interviews: professional interviewers target respondents in the high street.
- Hall tests: these are similar to street interviews, but respondents are asked to come into a hall for the interview. These are very useful for testing a product or ad.
- Personal interviews: the interviewer interviews one person, a couple or a group of friends.
- Focus group interviews: groups of six–ten people are interviewed together. The idea is to generate a discussion.

Observation methods

- Mystery shopping: the researcher pretends to be a consumer in order to evaluate the service they receive.
- In-store observation: survey or electronic surveillance to track consumer behaviour.

Do it!

Write a brief questionnaire to compare attitudes towards two different brands of soft drinks. You need to find out which brand questionnaire respondents usually buy and why they choose that particular brand. See if you can find out whether they are influenced by advertising when it comes to making a choice about which brand to buy.

Pilot the questionnaire by asking a group of your classmates to complete the questionnaire. Consider whether you got all the information that you required or whether you could have improved your questionnaire. Can you think of other ways that you could have got the same information?

The campaign planning cycle

WHERE ARE
WE NOW?

WHERE DO
WE WANT
TO BE?

DID WE GET
THERE?

HOW DO
WE GET
THERE?

Having received the brief from the client, the agency must now take all the knowledge that they have and use it to develop a campaign that will meet the requirements of the brief. They need to look closely at all the information they have been given and understand what it really means. The agency must also identify any gaps in their knowledge that can be filled through market research.

The fundamental questions that typify the campaign planning cycle are shown in the diagram opposite. They mirror the information supplied by the client brief, but the key element added by the agency is under the heading 'How do we get there?'. This is a cyclical model – once the campaign's effectiveness has been evaluated under the heading 'Did we get there?', this information is fed into the next campaign to ensure the 'Where are we now?' section always remains current.

Where are we now?

As has been mentioned, the client will supply much of this information in the client brief. The client should know all the answers to the questions outlined below through their own market research, but the agency may commission additional research to fill any knowledge gaps. The questions outlined under the headings below typify the information needed by the agency to be able to come up with credible campaign strategies.

Market share
• How do sales compare with those of competitors?

Key competitors
• Who are they?
• What is their market share?
• What is their advertising expenditure?
• How great is there media presence?

Position in the market
• How is the product/brand differentiated from key competitors?
• How do customers view the company/product/brand?

Brand awareness
• How high is spontaneous awareness of the brand (without naming it, e.g. name a brand of coffee)?
• How high is prompted awareness of the brand (when it is named, e.g. have you heard of Nescafé Gold Blend)?

Where do we want to be?

The basis of this information can be found in the client brief. The agency will consider what the client wants to achieve and will evaluate whether the objectives are practical and achievable in a single campaign.

Fundamental to this planning process is a clear understanding of the brand's current position. What do consumers actually think of the brand, as opposed to what the client believes that they think? Planners need to understand consumers' perceptions, both positive and negative, to decide what to do next. Brand position refers to the functional (or rational) elements of the brand, product or service in terms of what it does, and the consumer needs that the brand, product or service satisfies. It also refers to the emotional elements of the brand, product or service, in terms of the benefits that it offers.

Love life (below)

Diet Coke with cherry can trade off the brand heritage of Coca Cola, but it also needs to find its own brand position among the younger target market that it's aimed at.

Client: The Coca Cola Company / Agency: Vallance Carruthers Coleman Priest / Creative Directors: Rooney Carruthers and Mark Orbine / Copywriter: John McLaughlin / Production Company: Moon / Director: Mike Stephenson

How do we get there?

At this point in the planning process the agency really adds value for the client as they produce an advertising and media strategy to meet the objectives outlined in the client brief. Using their knowledge of the target audience, account planners will generate an advertising strategy based on four key factors.

Category need

Sometimes companies launch new products that don't fit within an existing category of products or services. This is a great opportunity, but the company not only has to establish the product, they also have to explain the benefits of this new category so people can understand why they might need the product. A great example of this is the launch of Tetley teabags in 1963. At the time, teabags were unheard of so Tetley had to sell in the whole idea of using tea in a bag at the same time as promoting their own brand.

Brand awareness

Brand awareness can be sub-divided into brand recall and brand recognition. If a client wants consumers to remember the brand when they need a product, then the agency needs to nurture brand recall. The consumer needs to think of a particular chocolate bar (not just a bar of chocolate), before they enter the shop and go in with the purpose of buying it. If the client wants the consumer to recognise their chocolate bar when they are in a shop and then decide to buy it, the agency may choose to focus on brand recognition.

Brand attitude

The consumer's attitude to the brand is a complex mix of their beliefs about the brand and their perceptions of the benefits associated with the brand. Different strategies can be employed to shift consumer attitudes related to the positioning of the brand such as aligning the brand with a credible celebrity as Walkers Crisps did with Gary Lineker, or linking advertising and sponsorship as Mastercard has on a global scale.

Brand usage

Strategies can be employed to encourage increased use of a product by positioning it as appropriate in different settings or at different times of the day. For example, Kellogg's Special K recently launched their 'Drop a Jean Size in two Weeks' campaign, suggesting that you should have a bowl of cereal at breakfast and lunch as part of a weight loss plan. This encouraged increased consumption of the product and endorsed its position as a healthy breakfast option.

While the advertising strategy is being developed, the media planning department will be considering the most appropriate media for the target audience. Advertising can only be effective if it reaches the people that it is intended to reach. The best advertising strategy in the world will be ineffective if the right target audience is not exposed to it in the right media.

Are you a noodlehead? (above and opposite)

This great campaign gets the message across that Super Noodles go with just about anything. Sometimes you need to remind consumers about how they can use a product or category or you can get them to buy more of your product if you can encourage different uses.

Client: Campbell's / Product: Batchelor's Super Noodles block / Agency: Delaney Lund Knox Warren & Partners / Copywriter: James Hodge / Art Director: Richard Fox / Photographer: Mark Polyblank

Did we get there?

There are constant debates in the advertising industry about campaign evaluation. Clients are under pressure to see a return on their advertising investment and even seek to remunerate agencies based on the performance of the campaign. Agencies recognise the need for their campaigns to achieve objectives, but are often resistant to the idea that the aim of advertising is to sell. They are more likely to see advertising as a long-term investment in the brand rather than a short-term sales fix.

Brand awareness is often used as an evaluative benchmark and it is tracked before and after campaigns to see if a wider audience is now aware of the brand. However, being aware of a product does not necessarily mean that a consumer will buy it. The related attitude to the brand and the consumer's purchase intention is obviously important.

Many brands that you see advertised today have been around for years. The advertising is intended to remind people and to encourage them to remain loyal to the brand. In these cases, sales can be a useful benchmark – effective campaigns can ensure that sales levels are maintained if not increased, and can certainly avoid a reduction in sales.

Campaign planning is a cyclical process and the final evaluation of the campaign will be used to enhance the next phase of activity. If a strategy has worked well then it is likely to be used again, in some form, in the next campaign.

Do it!

This chapter has looked at campaign development from the client brief up to the development of the creative brief, which will be considered in Chapter 3, The creative brief. It's important to remember the difference between the client brief and the creative brief – one articulates what the client needs to achieve and the other how the agency plans to achieve those objectives. The stages in between are where the agency can really add value as they develop the advertising strategy that is right for that campaign.

List all the tasks that agencies undertake between the moment they receive the brief from the client up until the development of the creative brief.

CHAPTER 3
THE CREATIVE BRIEF

The role of the brief

An agency's account management and account planning teams will transform a client brief into a creative brief. Together they will develop an advertising strategy based on the information supplied in the client brief and the supplementary research undertaken. The campaign strategy is then articulated in the creative brief, which is approved by the client.

As the starting point of the creative process, the creative brief is paramount. The creative brief serves several different, but equally vital, functions. Firstly, it provides the creative team with important background information about the client, the brand, product or service, the target market and audiences. Secondly, the creative brief clarifies the aims and objectives of the advertising campaign and identifies the campaign's key issues; placing special focus on the advertising message or 'proposition'. Finally, the creative brief provides a means of formalising specific criteria and objectives in a way that both the client and the agency can understand and agree on.

What the creative brief provides

A good creative brief should be written in a way that stimulates creativity and promotes original ideas. Some briefs suggest routes that the creative team may wish to explore while others contain 'creative starters' or snippets of information that may trigger imaginative ways of looking at the problem. The creative brief allows the agency to check the strategic integrity of their ideas and assess whether all of the requirements outlined in the client brief have been achieved. However the creative brief is constructed, it should satisfy five key criteria:

An opening dialogue

The creative brief is the point at which the strategic process ends and the creative process begins. As such, it should open up a dialogue with the creative team that will not only provide important background information, but will also lend itself to further debate and the exploration of alternative routes.

A point of focus

The creative brief should answer two key questions; 'what do you want to say?', and 'who do you want to say it to?'. These answers will help anchor the creative team's ideas and prevent their concepts from drifting 'off brief'. The brief is not intended to constrain creativity, but instead help to guide it in the right direction, and as such it should be written in a way that is single minded without being too restrictive.

A contract

The creative brief serves as a statement of intent. It provides both the agency and the client with a common reference point of what has been agreed in terms of the advertising objectives, the form of media, the tone of voice, the message and audience for the message. The client will be expected to approve the brief before the creative work commences.

A checklist

The creative brief should clarify the campaign's objectives and deliverables (outcomes). In doing so any subsequent ideas and concepts that the creative team generate can be tested against these criteria to check that they fulfil the brief's requirements. When presenting ideas to the client, the agency can also use the brief as a means of demonstrating to the client that their ideas fulfil its requirements.

And finally...

The brief should be seen as a framework from which creativity can emerge. At the same time, it is important that the brief does not channel the creative team too narrowly towards a certain way of thinking about the brand, product or service. There needs to be enough room for the imagination to wander and for the creative team to discover things about the brand that a more informed party may have missed or taken for granted. The brief needs to achieve a difficult balance and provide enough information to direct the creative team, without actually leading them.

One sock (left)

First Direct won a Silver DMA Award for Creativity in 2005 for this pack. They were trying to encourage customers to switch from the bigger banks by showing how thoughtful and flexible they are. They sent out prospects (prospective customers) one black sock to make up a pair with the inevitable odd sock left over after doing the laundry.

Client: First Direct / Agency: Craik Jones Watson Mitchell Voelkel / Creatives: Rebecca Rae, Olu Falola, Caroline Parkes, Annabel Wright, Louise MacLean

Do it!

Imagine that you are the brand. Now write a brief for yourself.

You must decide who your target audience is and what your objectives are. Are you trying to get a job? A place on a course? New business? Once you know what your objective is, start formulating the best strategy for achieving this and decide the role that advertising will play. Then you're ready to write the creative brief. Remember to be single-minded and focus on a clear proposition: what is the most important thing you want your audience to remember and take away from your advertisement?

Developing the brief

Before the creative brief can be formulated, the objectives of the advertising campaign have to be identified, together with a strategy for achieving those objectives. It is important to remember that the advertising medium itself is only one part of the communication strategy, which in turn is part of the overall marketing strategy. As such, the broader marketing strategy has to be considered before the creative brief can be formulated.

At the core of the advertising strategy is the need to identify who the advertisement is talking to and what it will want to say to them. In order to answer these questions the account planning team will undertake a process of analysis called 'the planning cycle' (see The campaign planning cycle, p.78). This examines the marketplace in which the brand operates, the current brand position in that market, the future positioning (where it could be), and how the brand is going to get there.

www.shepherdneame.co.uk   The BOTTLE of BRITAIN

Who are you talking to?

The marketing plan will normally define the target audience in purely demographic terms, for example 'married women aged between 30–50'. It is the account planning team's task to translate this demographic profile into a more vivid and descriptive snapshot of the target audience; the people that the advertising will address. This process brings the image of the target audience to life and provides the creative team with a clearer idea of who they are talking to. For example, the account planning team's description of the same target audience may be: 'married women aged 30–50 who would love to buy the brand, but have always thought that they cannot justify paying such a high price for it. They see the brand as stylish and fashionable and have a circle of friends that are equally impressed by the brand and what it stands for'.

The bottle of Britain (below)

This series of posters and press ads knows exactly who their target audience are and their tone of voice reflects this assumption.

Client: Shepherd Neame 'Spitfire' beer / Agency: RPM3 / Creative Director: Russell Wailes / Creative team: Ian Pittams and Denis Williams

What do you want to say?

What you choose to say about the brand is of primary importance. Only when you have decided exactly what it is you want to say can you determine how you are going to say it. There may be many different things that can be said about the brand, product or service, and a range of benefits that can be highlighted, but ultimately the team needs to be disciplined enough to settle for the one thing that is most likely to help achieve the advertising objectives. Saying too much will end up either diluting or confusing the core message, so it is vital that the team is single-minded about what they want the advertisements to tell people. That way, the creative team will have more focus and be more likely to develop a strong idea that is 'campaignable', i.e. effective across a wide range of media. The task of identifying exactly what the advertisement should say is one that can generate a very useful and productive dialogue between account planners and an agency's creative team. It is however the creative team that is responsible for transforming this statement or proposition into a selling idea.

Dyson and Smart car (below and below right)

There are a few brands that undoubtedly do have a USP, but open access to the technology means that before long competing brands offer the same benefits.

Images reproduced courtesy of Dyson Ltd., and DaimlerChrysler UK Ltd.

Unique selling proposition

The unique selling proposition (USP) is the single most important thing that the agency and the client want the audience to remember once they have seen or heard the advertisement. Rosser Reeves of the Ted Bates advertising agency developed the concept of a USP in the 1950s. The basic premise of the USP was that every brand had something unique about it that made it distinctive from its competitors. This unique element could be turned into a benefit and used as a proposition to sell the brand.

While the USP may have been an effective advertising tool for many brands in the 1950s and 1960s, there are very few brands today that are, in a traditional sense, really unique from the competition. Nowadays most competing brands tend to be equally matched in terms of quality, performance and technical specifications (a phenomenon sometimes referred to as 'market convergence'). However, this does not exclude one brand from developing a 'personality' that is very different to that of a competing brand. Building a strong brand is all about developing a strong, clearly defined personality for that brand; one that the consumer can relate to and ultimately like. Marketing, design and advertising have a large role to play in defining that personality and developing a brand identity which is not only true to the brand, but is also very distinctive from the competition. Thus the reason for buying one brand over another is more often an emotional response based on personal involvement and feelings for the brand, as opposed to a rational one which may consider specific benefits that one brand offers over the other.

Emotional selling proposition

The concept of the USP has been largely replaced by another principle, which John Bartle, Managing Director of Bartle Bogle Hegarty, has dubbed the emotional selling proposition (ESP). For example, when Mr Kipling advertisements announce that the brand bakes 'exceedingly good cakes', a range of images, words, scripts and sounds, which are intended to appeal to our emotions, all support the claim. It would be very difficult to prove that Mr Kipling's cakes are in fact better than the other leading brands of cake, but the marketing communication triggers connotations that appeal to the audience on an emotional level, and in doing so the brand establishes a personal connection with them.

In the absence of a specific unique benefit (a USP) inherent in the brand itself, the ESP is based on the uniqueness that is created by the advertising and marketing campaign. At the core of the ESP is a 'brand truth', an aspect of the brand often revealed in research. The brand truth might be that most consumers claim the brand makes them feel young again, or it reassures them, or they feel it represents top quality or that it has a better taste than similar brands... and so on. Expressing that thought in a unique and unexpected way is central to a successful campaign.

Finding something different to say about a brand that operates in a competitive market, where all the competitors look, taste and cost the same, is a real test of creativity. As a brand, Tango had found little to differentiate itself from the numerous other soft drink brands available. That was until the advertising agency HHCL were hired to turn things around. The advertising strategy formulated by the agency was to create an advertising campaign for Tango that owed more in style and content to lager advertising than soft drink advertisements. The result was something totally new and unexpected. The first new wave of Tango television commercials featured a bald, overweight, orange man who crept up on an unsuspecting Tango drinker and slapped them across the face. The symbolic representation of the 'hit of the Tango taste' may have been lost on some viewers, but the memorability generated by the novel approach helped make Tango stand out from all of its competitors. The brand's packaging reflected this repositioning. Al Young (former Creative Director of HHCL) said of the campaign, 'It's about finding the right kind of wrongness'.

Finding something original to say about the brand involves courage on the part of the client and the agency. Originality implies that the idea has not been tried or tested before, and consequently the outcomes are unknown. As Al Young is quick to point out: 'When you're trying to create something original, where there is no blueprint for success, there is always a risk that you will fail. It's inevitable that sometimes you'll end up finding the wrong kind of wrongness instead'.

Tango (below)

The big difference may be not what you say, but how you say it. When there is little real product benefit to differentiate one brand from its competition, then it is the unique way that you market the brand that makes the difference.

Image reproduced courtesy of Britvic Soft Drinks Ltd.

The content of the brief

The creative brief should be written in simple terms, not jargon or marketing 'speak'. Although the format of the brief tends to vary from agency to agency, the general content normally includes nine key areas of information.

Background

This provides the creative team with the fundamental 'need to know' information about the brand, product or service. It may also include information on past and present advertising communications, market conditions, competitors and perceptions of the brand. The background information should also outline the advertising problem itself, thus establishing a reason for the advertising.

Objectives

Sometimes referred to as the role of advertising, this section essentially outlines what exactly needs to be achieved through the advertising campaign. It could be to prompt an increase in sales or awareness of the brand. It could be to educate or inform people of something. It could be to encourage a change of heart or a shift in behaviour of some kind. It could be to enhance recruitment, sales enquiries, or simply generate interest. Whatever the objectives are, it is important that they are expressed in a clear way so that everyone has a common understanding of what needs to be achieved.

Target audience

Here, the agency defines the people they are addressing with the advertising communication. The brief should include information that gives some insight into the personality and behaviour of the target audience. It is very important that the creative team has a clear idea of who the members of their target audience are; their lifestyles, interests, pursuits, beliefs, what jobs they have, their expectations and how they generally tend to act or think. This can be difficult if the audience is very diverse in nature, but it is essential if the right proposition is to be reached.

BRIEF DATE	7th August	CLIENT	Depaul Trust	
INTERNAL REVIEW	15th September	BRAND	Depaul Trust	PRODUCT Depaul Trust
CLIENT PRESENTATION	TBC	MEDIA/CHANNEL(S)	Open	
BUDGET	Very small	COPY DEADLINE	N/A	

PUBLICIS

What does this brand stand for?	Preventing Homelessness.
What's the business problem or opportunity here?	Unlike other 'homeless charities, the Depaul Trust acts on the causes not just the consequences of homelessness for young people. This includes education, training, sports and post prison mentoring- they also offer roots over heads when required. The opportunity is to greatly increase the number of private donations to enable further work to be undertaken.
What's the role of communications in answering it?	Communications must generate awareness of the brand and vitally, increase understanding of Depaul in a way which inspires empathy with their work and willingness to donate.
Who are we talking to?	All private donors, people like you and me who earn money and have enough to give a small amount each month.
In what moment or mindset are we talking to them?	We need to identify the right media at the right time to standout and connect with people. Depaul have VERY limited funds, so we need to wring every penny out of any ads we run.
What do they currently think or feel about us?	Most people don't know of or anything about the Depaul Trust (hampered by the name). People have their 'favourite' charity or cause and might give to it, e.g. cancer research, but the market is dominated by the bigger spending charities.
What do we want them to think, feel (and therefore do)?	The Depaul Trust is a pioneering homeless charity which prevents homelessness through tackling its causes and consequences among young disadvantaged adults.
What's the one thing we can say to achieve this?	Depaul believes that the best way to keep people off the streets, is to prevent them getting there in the first place.

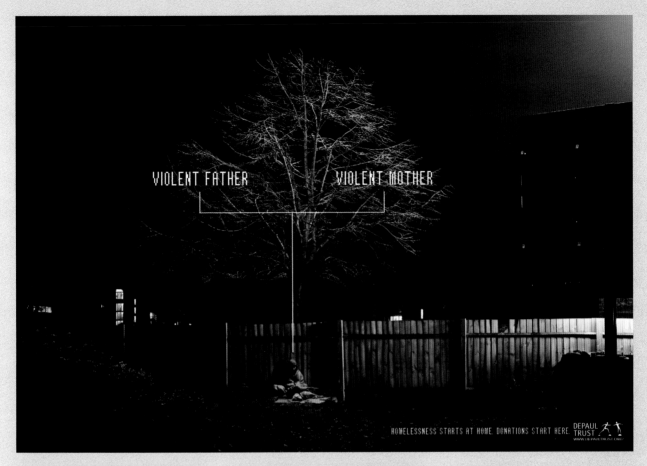

VIOLENT FATHER   VIOLENT MOTHER

HOMELESSNESS STARTS AT HOME. DONATIONS START HERE.   DEPAUL TRUST

Depaul Trust script (opposite) and execution (this page)

This Publicis campaign dramatises the root causes of homelessness, offering Londoners a compelling reason to donate to the Depaul Trust.

Client: Depaul Trust / Agency: Publicis UK / Creative Director: Nik Studzinski / Art Directors/Copywriters: Andrew Petch and Cameron Blackley / Photographer: Ernst Fischer

The proposition

This is the advertising message itself, as some agencies prefer to define it: 'the single most important thing you want people to remember when they see you advertisement'. The proposition should be single-minded and focused. It should provide the reader or viewer with the reason why he or she should buy the client's product or service.

There may be many features and benefits that could be used to help sell a brand, but the agency needs to decide which of those benefits is the single most important one; the one that is most likely to interest the target audience. One senior creative used to demonstrate this to advertising students by throwing a tennis ball into groups that would attend his talks and lectures. One student in the audience would invariably catch the ball and hurl it back. The creative would then instruct the student to try catching the ball again. However, this time the creative would throw several balls at the student, who would predictably catch none. The meaning of this metaphorical exercise is clear: 'If you try to communicate too much information, you risk communicating nothing'. The truth of the matter is that in a society where the average person is exposed to thousands of advertisements a day, the advertising message has to cut through a great deal of virtual 'noise'. The readers or viewers are more likely to recall a single strong reason to buy the product, than a list of all the other things that the product can do or offer them.

Spiderman (this page)

This ad for Spiderman pasta shapes was published in consumer magazines. Why do you think this media was chosen?

Client: Heinz / Agency: Leo Burnett / Art Directors/Copywriters: Nick Pringle and Clark Edwards / Photographer: Kelvin Murray

How do you want the audience to react?

This information may or may not be included as part of the advertising objectives. Essentially, it outlines how the agency wants the target audience to react to the campaign and what they want them to think or do after they have seen the advertising.

Substantiation (or support)

This part of the brief lists the reasons why the audience should believe the proposition. It is the evidence that supports the claim made by your advertisement. So whether it is a promise that this detergent will clean clothes better or that a particular mobile phone offers the cheapest deal, the audience needs to have a good reason to believe the advertisement. The evidence may be facts and figures about the brand, such as how it performs, how popular it is, how people perceive it or how it compares with its competition. If the agency has to communicate something amazing about the client's product or brand, they will need to do so in a way that will convince even the most sceptical consumer. The creative team will be responsible for expressing this information in an original and memorable way, to make the advertising claim or proposition believable.

Tone of voice

The 'tone of voice' refers to the overall mood projected by the advertisement, for example, is it necessary to be humorous, light-hearted, fun, serious, authoritative, confident or knowledgeable? There are of course many different tones of voice you can use, which provide you with an opportunity to emphasise a particular aspect of the brand or make a connection with the consumer.

Requirements

This section lists the specific media needed to communicate your proposition to your target audience. These items might range from press or magazine advertisements and posters to radio or television commercials and internet banners. This part of the brief will specify the likely choice and size of media.

Mandatories

This section of the brief, covering mandatories (or executional considerations) specifies any elements that have to be included in the advertisements or commercials. Typically these may include items such as the client's logo, slogan, website address, telephone number or other contact details or any legally required information. The client's corporate house style will also have to be considered. The use of certain typestyles, colours, images and the general look and style of the advertising may be stipulated by corporate or brand guidelines.

Do it!

Look at the ads opposite and try to work out what was in the creative brief. Then answer the following questions:

1. Who are the ads talking to?

2. What do they want the audience to think or do?

3. What is the proposition?

4. What are the objectives?

5. What is the tone of voice?

CHAPTER 4
THE CREATIVE CONCEPT

The creative team

At the heart of every successful advertising campaign is the creative concept. The task of having an original concept, and a range of ideas allied to this concept, is in the hands of the creative team. The best creative teams have the capacity to be both original and fluent when it comes to generating such ideas. In other words, it is not just about having a novel idea… it's about having lots of them!

Different creative teams, and individuals within those teams, often develop their own methods for having ideas. What works for one team may not work for another. However, there are certain things that can be done to help this process and stimulate ideas.

This chapter will endeavour to offer advice, hints and suggestions on how to get from the brief to the idea. In order to do this, the chapter addresses the reader as a member of the creative team and provides guidance and tips on generating ideas, visualising those ideas and writing good headlines and copy to accompany them.

Who are the creative team?

An agency's creative team is responsible for the origination of advertising ideas and concepts from a creative brief supplied by the planner and account team. Traditionally this team was made up of an art director and copywriter. This model was developed in the 1960s by the New York agency Doyle Dane Bernbach, and soon become an industry standard.

In the modern advertising agency, members of the creative team have to be ideas people, solving clients' advertising problems. This will be achieved by having a thorough understanding of consumer behaviour and the many varied media channels available to the advertiser to reach fragmented target audiences.

Nowadays, the traditional roles within a creative team have also become blurred; the art director is as likely the think up a headline as the copywriters will the visual. However, it is good practice for any aspiring creative team to work to each others' strengths. One of the team should be able to write good copy while the other should have skills in design, layout and visualising. Improving these transferable skills will be useful when freelancing and working in smaller agencies, where teams will be expected to carry out more of the work themselves.

Creative team (this page)

Chris Spore and Nick Cooper paired up as a creative team whilst studying advertising at university. After graduating, and following more than a year of job searching, they were offered the opportunity to work for leading DM agency Rapp Collins. Since joining Rapp Collins they have worked on accounts such as Wannado and the NSPCC.

What makes a good creative team?

'First and foremost you've got to get along, you've both got to care about the work you produce and care about being original'.
Dan Warner, copywriter at Rainey, Kelly, Campbell, Roalfe / Y&R

The most successful creative teams share a passion for advertising and aspire to producing the very best creative work for their portfolio. This desire for success often involves working intensively together on difficult briefs for long hours, so it helps if members of the team like one another and share a sense of humour. In an agency, all the creative work produced has to be approved by the creative director before it is presented to the client, consequently many ideas are rejected or require further development on the concept. It is important to learn to use this criticism constructively, so that better work can be produced in the future.

Creative teams have often been compared to magpies, continually collecting ideas, pictures, cuttings from magazines and anything else they feel is worth storing away, providing creative inspiration that can then be drawn upon at a later date. Dean Iqbal, an art director with Rainey Kelly Campbell Roalfe / Y&R sees it as '…very important. Doing 'new things' is one way to maintain awareness'. Visits to the cinema, theatre, art galleries and listening to popular, classical, world and jazz music can inspire a poster visual or a soundtrack for a TV commercial script. Reading all types of newspapers, magazines and comics can offer valuable insights into how people of different ages and social class think and behave. As the award-winning art director Graham Fink wisely points out, 'If you are "too cool", you may miss out on something important'.

Maureen 118212 (below)

Southampton Solent University's first class graduate Simon Cenamor and his creative partner Raymond Chan met at Graham Fink's 'Artschool' during a creative team matchmaking event. After three months working on various briefs together they found a placement with Leith London. Since working there they have produced campaigns for Goodfella's pizzas, The Edinburgh Dungeon and the Maureen 118212 poster campaign featured here.

Client: 118212 (Maureen) / Agency: Leith London / Art Director: Raymond Chan / Copywriter: Simon Cenamor

Research and familiarisation

The way the creative brief is written and its content can be an important trigger for your ideas and will also provide an important point of focus for you in terms of advertising objectives; who you are talking to, what you want to say to them, and how you want them to respond. For this reason it is best to keep referring back to the brief every so often during the creative process to make sure that you are staying on track. When you have a good idea and start getting excited about it, it is very easy to get diverted from the purpose of the advertising.

The key to having a great idea is the preparation that you put into the initial stages of this process. This preparation involves finding out as much information as you can about the product (or service) and the various stakeholders; from the people that make or sell the product, to those who may purchase or use it. At the same time you need to familiarise yourself with the product; go to the factory where it is made, talk to the people who make it, talk to the people who sell it or use it, try using it yourself for a while and test its limitations. There are countless ways you can extend your experience and knowledge of the product. Only then can you really start talking about it to an advertising audience.

Find interesting facts or snippets

It is true to say that 'facts sell, generalisations don't'. You will need to discover interesting facts about the product or service, which are relevant to the advertising proposition itself. In order for those facts to be interesting, they have to be things that the audience is unaware of. Sometimes these facts may be trivial observations that have remained unnoticed before, but when highlighted they communicate the advertising proposition in a novel, unexpected and powerful way.

During the 1960s, Rolls Royce wanted to let potential customers know just how quiet the Rolls Royce engine was. They ran print advertisements showing the car driving past and a headline that read: 'At 60 miles an hour the loudest noise in this new Rolls Royce comes from the electric clock'. The advertisement could have just shown a picture of the car with a headline that read: 'it's as quiet as a mouse', but that would have been boring!

Around the same time, the company ran a campaign of press advertisements that depicted the manufacturing stages the car underwent in the factory. This provided an opportunity to show the car in a series of unusual photographs, which were considerably more interesting that the conventional stock advertising shot that most people had come to expect from car manufacturers. One photograph showed a man in a suit, climbing into the boot of the vehicle with a headline that posed the question 'why?'. The advertisement's body copy revealed that this man's job involved travelling in the boot of the finished car to listen for rattles and other problematic noises. Not only was this an interesting fact discovered through research into the manufacture of the car, but it was a totally unexpected means of commenting on the extra lengths the company were prepared to go in order to assure the quality of the product.

The unexpectedness or surprise that your headline or image creates is what will ultimately generate the greatest awareness and recall.

Get to know your audience

Remember that it is not only the product you need to be familiar with. You will need to have an in-depth knowledge of your audience too. This needs to go beyond the general demographic information such as age, gender, status and so on. It encompasses considerations such as; how they talk, what kind of issues are important to them, what jobs they have, what views and opinions they harbour (about your client's product and life in general), what their needs and desires are, the lifestyle they lead and the lifestyle they may aspire to. Some of this information may be in the brief, but the rest of it you will need to discover for yourself. This may not be an easy task, particularly if your audience is a sector of the population with whom you have had little contact or knowledge of in the past.

If you can, focus on someone you personally know who falls within the same target group. How would you talk to that person? What would really interest them? What would get their attention and capture their imagination? In a sense, you should be thinking in terms of communicating with a single person, rather than a mass audience. That way you are more likely to address the audience in a more personal 'one-to-one' way, rather than a general message for a general audience. In some cases you may need to go further in order to really develop a sense of empathy for your audience. If at all possible, put yourself in their shoes for a while and try to see the product you are advertising or the issue you are promoting from their perspective. It is only when you can convince your audience that you understand their problems, issues or viewpoints that they may start listening to what you have to say.

Multiple Sclerosis (above)
Familiarisation with the problem and conveying it in an interesting and compelling manner is the key to the success of this ad.

Client: MS Society / Agency: Saatchi & Saatchi / Art Director: Colin Jones / Copywriter: Michael Campbell

Do it!

When you compare like-for-like products, there is often very little to differentiate one from another. Sometimes you have to look deeper to find something different to say about the brand that is interesting and provides a new angle.

1. Choose a well-known beer or petrol brand and find something different to say about the way the product is sourced, manufactured, treated, sold, used or consumed. Once you have done this, look at how this information can be used to express a brand proposition and provides a reason for someone to buy it.

2. Choose any advertising campaign that is currently running (but not directly targeted at you) and visualise the target audience you think the campaign is aimed at. What do they feel strongly about? What do they think about the brand? Think about what other questions you could ask to really understand your audience.

Idea generation (ideation)

The secret to having good ideas is to have lots of ideas to choose from. The more ideas you have, the greater the chance that there will be a few 'winners' among them. Quantity equals quality, so don't hold back and pre-judge your ideas, just have lots of them – the wilder the better! Wild ideas may be unusable in their raw state, but they can provide a springboard to a better idea as they can help you to see things from a different perspective.

Seeing the creative problem with 'fresh eyes' is a prerequisite for producing a concept that will present the advertising proposition in an original and memorable way. It may be that your first idea turns out to be your best one, but don't count on it. When you have that great idea at the outset, put it away and move on to have another one, and another. Then at the end of the day you can pick and choose. Don't be too precious about your ideas either. It's easy to get carried away with a creative idea and forget the original objective in the brief or miss the bigger picture. Once you have had all those wonderful wild and creative ideas, then (and only then) it's time to take stock and test them against the requirements of the brief.

It's essential that the advertising proposition comes across clearly and single-mindedly. Try to be objective when you are judging your own ideas and listen to what other people have to say about them. The most valuable advertising ideas are those that are not just original and on brief, but those that are campaignable and have a central concept or theme that can run over several advertisements in different media. Often the best ideas are the simplest ones. In fact your great idea may be so simple, you will wonder why it has not been used already.

This is what happens when a fly lands on your food. Flies can't eat solid food, so to soften it up they vomit on it. Then they stamp the vomit in until it's a liquid, usually stamping in a few germs for good measure. Then when it's good and runny they suck it all back again, probably dropping some excrement at the same time. And then, when they've finished eating, it's your turn.

Cover food. Cover eating and drinking utensils. Cover dustbins.
The Health Education Council

Taking them by surprise

Of course there is another reason why it is important to develop an understanding of your audience. If you can understand how they think and what things are likely to trigger certain responses or reactions from them, you can use this knowledge to create surprise. A common element of all great advertising ideas or concepts is the element of surprise or unexpectedness that may be incorporated in different aspects of the concept, ranging from tone and style, to unusual visual metaphors or images that are not normally associated with the particular product category. Alternatively, it could just be an unusual way of showing a familiar scene or event. Either way, there is an element of surprise and unexpectedness involved. However, in order to build this element into your idea, you must first understand what your audience *expects* to see.

What happens when a fly lands on your food? (opposite)

By thoroughly researching their client's business copywriters can discover interesting facts or snippets, which may be the start of an advertising idea. This 1970s Health Education Council poster, written by a young Charles Saatchi, was inspired by government literature of the day.

Client: The Health Education Council (UK) / Agency: Saatchi & Saatchi / Art Director: John Hegarty / Copywriters: Charles Saatchi and Michael Coughlan Reproduced under the terms of the Click-Use Licence

Bullet hole (this page)

A single bullet hole runs through the whole of *Vibe* magazine, graphically illustrating how many people are affected by gun crime in London. Left in barber shops across selected boroughs of London, this direct ad effectively promoted how police initiative Operation Trident can help stop shootings in London's black community.

Client: Metropolitan Police Services / Agency: Miles Calcraft Briginshaw Duffy / Art Director: Dave Hobbs / Copywriter: Richard Stoney / Typographer: Kerry Roper / Creative Directors: Paul Briginshaw, Malcolm Duffy Image supplied courtesy of the D&AD Global Awards (Direct Mail: Public services and charities: Silver Award, 2005)

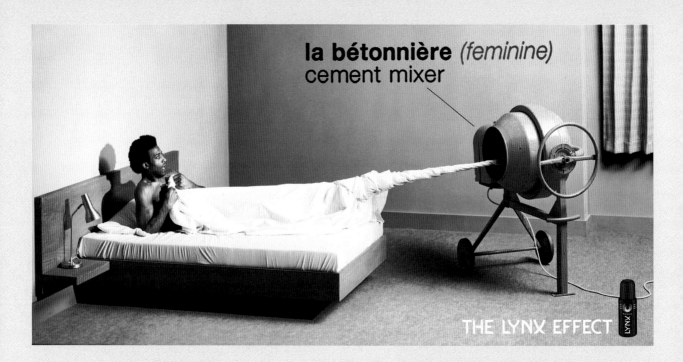

la **bétonnière** *(feminine)*
cement mixer

THE LYNX EFFECT

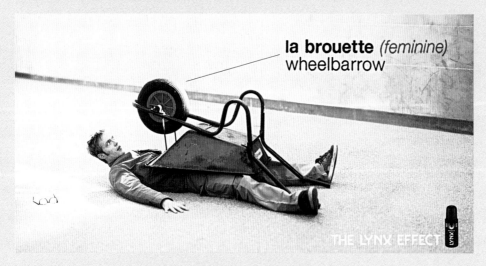

la **brouette** *(feminine)*
wheelbarrow

THE LYNX EFFECT

**Cement mixer. Wheelbarrow.
(this page)**
These brilliantly surreal ads appear
at first glance too sophisticated for
the target audience.

Client: Lynx/ Agency: Bartle Bogle
Hegarty UK / Producer: Nik Upton /
Photographer: Malcolm Venville /
Creative Team: Rosie Arnold, Dave
Monk, Matt Waller

The comedian

It is no coincidence that some of the greatest and most memorable advertising ideas and campaigns use humour to get their message across. In fact, when it comes to making a connection with an audience, the way a stand-up comedian performs is a lesson for all advertising creatives. A comedian knows the audience well enough to lead their thought in a particular direction; he or she can then present them with a punchline that is unexpected and triggers laughter in much the same way that an unexpected advertising headline or visual prompts a sense of discovery and realisation.

Be observant

Observe human nature. Look at how people react in certain situations. What things, events or experiences trigger emotions such as happiness, sadness, fear, disgust, despair, joy, greed or envy? Ask yourself why those things trigger those reactions and you may discover a way to trigger the desired response from your audience. Tap into your own experiences, which may then be shared with members of that audience. Common experiences are often a way to connect with your audience and show that you understand them. If you can get them nodding and saying to themselves, 'Yes, I feel like that sometimes', then you have them listening to you.

Photobooth (above)

This simple and hilarious gag set in a photographic booth re-enacts a scenario well known to anybody who has used them. The camera always flashes at the wrong time – either you are looking the wrong way or you have both eyes closed! This script became part of the successful 'Happiness is a cigar called Hamlet' campaign.

Client: Hamlet / Agency: CDP-Travissully / Director: Graham Rose / Creative team: Rowan Dean, Philip Differ, Garry Horner
(Image used with kind permission of CDP-Travissully)

Isn't it time you got your own place? (right)

Observations of familiar scenes, or experiences, can help communicate the message in an unexpected and amusing way.

Client: Independent Newspapers (Saturday Star property guide) / Agency: TBWA Hunt Lascaris / Creative Director: Tony Granger / Art Directors/Copywriters: Mariana O'Kelly and Frances Luckin / Photographer: Jakob Doman / Typographer: Mariana O'Kelly

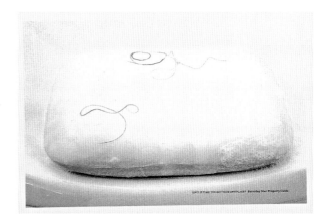

Keep a notebook

Get in the habit of recording any useful observations, ideas and discoveries. They may have no immediate relevance, but the fact that you found them interesting means that someone else is likely to be interested as well. Keep an 'ideas' notebook. This could become the first place to go when you are looking for inspiration or stimulus at a later stage, or for another project or creative brief.

Have lots of ideas

Often our first ideas can end up being our best idea. Try not to let a good idea get in the way of you having an even better one. When you have a good idea, bank it! Put it away and move on to have another idea. That way you will be sure to generate lots of different ideas and have plenty to choose from at the end of the day. It is very easy to fall in love with your first idea, particularly if it took a lot of hard work and time getting there. The capacity to explore different routes and approaches, and not become too fixed or attached to a single one, is the sign of a creative thinker.

Ideas notebook (below)
Many advertising creatives keep ideas notebooks, storing up observations and thoughts for future use.

Test your ideas

Once you have a range of different ideas it is wise to evaluate and assess them. Just how good are they? Once again, the first move should be to revisit the creative brief and make sure that the solutions you have meet the specified requirements and criteria. It is no good having a great idea if it fails to communicate the advertising proposition, or addresses the wrong type of audience. You may be able to adjust the idea so that it fits the brief or save it for another day and another campaign. There are other ways to assess how great your idea is. One method is called the 'overnight test'. Sometimes the great idea you had late at night after hours of focused concentration, hard work and effort does not seem so great the next day. By pinning your idea on the wall and revisiting it the next day you will have a fresh view of it, and often a more objective one. Test the idea on your friends or family; particularly those that fall within the same population as your target audience. How do they react to your idea?

Wall of ideas (below)

Advertising students at Southampton Solent University sharing and appraising each others' ideas.

Do it!

Start to compile a list of observations on human nature and 'real life' events. These should be everyday scenes that many of us have witnessed or shared, but never thought to question or examine in any depth. For example, the experience of using a photo booth and all that involves: choosing between a pale blue or orange curtain for the background, working out which slot to put the money in, adjusting the seat height, anticipating when the flash is going to go off, waiting for the photographs, the lack of privacy and the generally unpleasing results. Such observations are rich material for comedians and advertising creatives because they are scenes that their respective audiences are familiar with. When replayed (and sometimes exaggerated), they can help establish a connection with that audience in a witty and memorable way.

Once you have a book full of observations, use them as stimulus for ideas when you tackle new advertising briefs. Can the event or occurrence you have noted be used to express the advertising proposition?

Copywriting

The way words combine and interact with images in advertising is a vital part of the communication process. In the case of a typical magazine advertisement, the first thing that the reader will see is the picture and headline, and so the more you can communicate in that first encounter, the better. The very last thing the reader will look at is the body copy, which they will only read if your headline and image, together with the other visual aspects of the advertisement, have kept them sufficiently interested to want to read on.

Headlines

The best headlines complement the image – rather than just describe what is happening in the picture, they add meaning to it. A headline can make the advertisement meaningful in a number of different ways. It can turn the image it accompanies into a powerful metaphor that may underline and strengthen the brand proposition.

The headline can change the context of an image, thus adding an unexpected quality to the advertisement. In these instances, the image may suggest one thing while the headline alters the meaning; confounding the expectations of the reader in a way that challenges any initial assumptions he or she has made.

Sometimes a headline can make use of double meanings, slang or colloquial terminology to communicate a message. In such cases it is important that the way language is used will be understood by the target audience. For instance, there is no point writing a headline based on a regional dialect if your target audience comes from a completely different country and culture. They simply will not understand the advertising message. Irony, subtlety and wit can be wasted if they are dependent on local understanding and knowledge that a majority of your audience are not privy to. Such a use however, when appropriate and directed at the right audience, can be both powerful and witty.

In all cases the headline should work with the image to complete the 'story'. In other words, the headline or the picture on its own may make little or no sense, but when they come together, the full meaning and message is expressed in a clear, powerful and memorable way. The most important thing is to let the two parts of the advertisement (headline and image) do their own part of the communication task. If the headline is working effectively with the image, the reader should not have to start reading the body copy to understand the proposition.

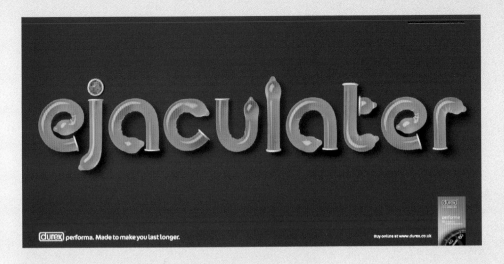

Ejaculater (left)

This witty, one word ad demonstrates perfectly the power of the advertising headline.

Client: Durex / Agency: McCann Erickson, Manchester / Art Director/Creative Director: Dave Price / Creative Partner/Copywriter: Neil Lancaster / Copywriter: Tim Reid / Photographer: Mike Parsons / Image Manipulator: Steve Reilly / Typographer: Karen Matthews

This way (left)

This gory adshell poster directed people (literally), to the Edinburgh Dungeon and was so successful that it led to a substantial increase in visits.

Client: Edinburgh Dungeon / Agency: Leith London / Art Director: Raymond Chan / Copywriter: Simon Cenamor

A good headline can explain a deliberately ambiguous image. By doing so, impact and memorability can often be achieved by 'teasing' the audience and playing visual games. The connection that the reader makes can be a simple one where the headline, together with the picture, instantly communicates the message. However, at the other extreme, the headline may provide a meaning or explanation that still requires the reader to make a leap of insight or solve a conundrum.

Getting the reader to make the connection

Some would argue that an advertising message should be communicated instantly, however some of the most memorable advertisements have become so by presenting the reader with a puzzle to solve. When the advertisement presents the reader with a visual conundrum, the interaction of working it out means that there can be a greater pay-off, or sense of reward when the puzzle is solved. This does not mean that the reader should be expected to struggle for hours to understand the advertisement, but that the audience should make the connection themselves. The advertisement should not have to explain it too overtly otherwise the effect would be similar to explaining a joke… it's never as funny!

Of course it is no good creating an advertisement that no one understands. At the end of the day, the message has to be clearly understood. The audience have to 'get it'. At the same time though, it is not always the case that the meaning has to be immediate. Making the reader think about it for a while is not necessarily a bad thing. While the reader is trying to make sense of it all, there is normally an element of branding going on inside the mind of that person (whether they are aware of it or not). In today's media-literate society, audiences are much better at decoding advertising messages than they were several decades ago. When combining headline and image in a way that requires the audience to make a connection, it is important to get the balance right; not too difficult and not too obvious for the reader to understand.

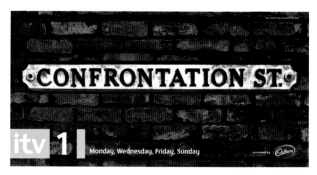

Revelation St. Confrontation St. Devastation St. (this page)
A clever play on words and strong art direction gives the reader a connection with this well-known English soap opera.

Client: ITV / Agency: M&C Saatchi / Creative Director: Graham Fink / Art Directors/Copywriters: Dan McCormack and Luke Boggins / Designer: Mark Henry

Finding the right headline

Writing great headlines is not a case of deciding what to say, it is a case of finding the best way to say it! The proposition given in the brief may define what the message is, but your headline has to help present that message in a way that is clear, compelling, unexpected and impactful. Great headlines can evoke equally great visual imagery.

When KFC (formerly Kentucky Fried Chicken) had to tell people that their brand of fried chicken was the tastiest around, the copy line: 'It's fingerlickin' good', was created to express that proposition. The real power of a line like this is the imagery it evokes in a few simple words. The headline itself is very visual and all it needs to accompany it is a mouth-watering photograph of the product itself. You do not need an image of someone licking their fingers after enjoying the product, as the copy line already conjures up that image in the mind's eye. To show it as well would lessen the effect.

A method of ensuring that headline and image work well together is to use the headline to describe something you can't see in the picture. This allows your reader's imagination to take over. When this happens, you're really starting to engage them.

The headline and any accompanying image should not only communicate the proposition, they should compel the reader to read on. It is a fact that only a few readers will ever bother reading the body copy of an advertisement, but if the advertisement contains any body copy, then your headline should lead them into this seamlessly. There are lots of ways that you can do this, but essentially it is all down to the level of interest or intrigue that your headline and image generate. One way you can do this is by offering a 'reward' for reading on. This reward could be the answer to a problem or question, a useful piece of information, or even the chance to win something. If you are writing for a poster, then it is important that your image provides the answer. If it is a press or magazine advertisement containing body copy, you may want to use the headline to prompt the reader to dip into it.

A Carrot. Eggs. (this page)
Clever and witty copy that also tells the consumer about price deals (without selling too hard!).

Client: Tesco / Agency: Red Brick Road / Art Director: Jason Lawes / Writer: Sam Cartmell / Photographer: Colin Campbell / Typographer: Marc Donaldson

Some dos and don'ts

Generally speaking, it is best to avoid clichés as your audience will have heard these time and time again. A cliché also tends to make your advertisement sound like an advertisement – and that is the last thing that you really want! Try to use exciting, action-oriented words as opposed to duller alternatives (just as long as they do not sound unnatural, decorative or contrived). For example, the word 'walk' could be replaced with 'amble', 'stroll', 'strut' or 'stride'. Each of these words are more 'visual' as they tell you more about the type of walk and provide an opportunity to increase the level of communication without increasing the length of the copy.

There are no hard and fast rules about how long or short a headline should be, but generally speaking, you should try to edit your headline down to something that is clear, simple and 'punchy'. You may find that a single word is enough, particularly if it is used well with a strong image. One way to edit down the headline is to make language as direct as possible. The headline: 'Try driving a new Ford today' is more dynamic when you change it to: 'Drive a new Ford today'.

Scrabble (above)

This London Underground poster poses a conundrum for waiting passengers. Will only readers of *The Economist* get it?

Client: *The Economist* / Agency: Abbot Mead Vickers BBDO / Copywriter: Tim Riley / Typographer: John Tisdall

Body copy

Good body copy starts in the middle – it carries on the 'story' from where the picture and headline left it. It does not bore the reader by going over information that they have already been presented with. That way it can continue to drive the pace and momentum created by a powerful headline, and get to the point quickly with a more efficient use of words.

It is generally not a good idea to start talking about the brand in the opening sentence of the body copy. Instead, try talking about the reader; his or her hopes, desires and aspirations. Show your audience that you understand them, the nature of the problem they may have or the difficulties they face, and that you can empathise with them. Only when you can show that you are interested in them, are they likely to show an interest in what you have to say.

Father's Day (below)

This David Abbott press ad tells the story of a son who recounts all the reasons why his dad deserves to be given a bottle of Chivas Regal as a Father's Day present. Why not write long copy ads for a change – use 'real life' situations as your inspiration.

Client: Chivas Regal / Agency: Abbott Mead Vickers BBDO Ltd. / Copywriter: David Abbott

Because I've known you all my life.

Because a red Rudge bicycle once made me the happiest boy on the street.

Because you let me play cricket on the lawn.

Because you used to dance in the kitchen with a tea-towel round your waist.

Because your cheque book was always busy on my behalf.

Because our house was always full of books and laughter.

Because of countless Saturday mornings you gave up to watch a small boy play rugby.

Because you never expected too much of me or let me get away with too little.

Because of all the nights you sat working at your desk while I lay sleeping in my bed.

Because you never embarrassed me by talking about the birds and the bees.

Because I know there's a faded newspaper clipping in your wallet about my scholarship.

Because you always made me polish the heels of my shoes as brightly as the toes.

Because you've remembered my birthday 38 times out of 38.

Because you still hug me when we meet.

Because you still buy my mother flowers.

Because you've more than your fair share of grey hairs and I know who helped put them there.

Because you're a marvellous grandfather.

Because you made my wife feel one of the family.

Because you wanted to go to McDonalds the last time I bought you lunch.

Because you've always been there when I've needed you.

Because you let me make my own mistakes and never once said "I told you so."

Because you still pretend you only need glasses for reading.

Because I don't say thank you as often as I should.

Because it's Father's Day.

Because if you don't deserve Chivas Regal, who does?

Write it as you would speak it

Use everyday language and talk to your audience as if you are talking to someone you know personally. That way, they are more likely to be open to what you have to say. Use observations and examples that people can relate to and a tone and style of language that they are familiar with. To this end, try to avoid using long words, complicated sentences or tenses just for the sake of sounding profound or aloof. If you really want to sound natural, then you have to seek simplicity and write your copy as you would expect to speak it. It is also good practice to generally steer clear from using unnaturally decorative, flowery language. Remember that you are not trying to impress the reader with your mastery of language or poetic ability. You are trying to sell the client's product.

Choose your words carefully and make every word count. You cannot say everything, so do not try. If the reader wants to know more they can send off for more details or the full technical specifications. It is your job to get them interested enough to do that.

Skin facts (below)

These humorous ads talk in a contemporary, ad lib style, in much the same way as a stand up comedian would deliver his or her lines.

Client: Unilever Malaysia / Advertising Agency: Ogilvy & Mather Malaysia / Creative Directors: Neil French and Sonal Dabral / Art Directors: Neil French and Brian Capel / Copywriter: Neil French

Skin Fact Nº21

The smoke from burning giraffe skin is used to treat nosebleeds among some tribes in Africa. These tribes always travel with a spare giraffe and a box of matches, in case they bump into a tree.

(Not really: I made that last bit up.)

(Dove is all <u>you</u> need to know about skincare.)

Skin Fact Nº28

The skin of the Crested Newt tastes horrid. This is said to be a defense against predators. On the other hand, since this wouldn't work until you were actually being eaten, it seems a somewhat questionable means of defense.

Revenge maybe.

(Dove is all <u>you</u> need to know about skincare.)

The strapline or slogan

The strapline (sometimes referred to as the endline, tagline or slogan), is normally a single word or short sentence which encapsulates the advertising message or proposition defined in the creative brief. The strapline also serves to unite all of the advertisements in a campaign under the umbrella of a single brand statement. The strapline: 'Just do it' becomes a powerful statement for Nike that expresses aspirational qualities of confidence, commitment and perseverance. All of the advertisements and commercials created for Nike subsequently project aspects of that strapline in their content.

Simple phonetic or alliterative qualities can make straplines or slogans catchier or more memorable. A campaign promoting butter ran the slogan: 'No buts, it's got to be butter', while a campaign for cream cakes ran with the line: 'naughty, but nice'. Ideally, the strapline should be short, simple and catchy, with strong positive connotations. You may even want to include the brand name in there somewhere to reinforce the branding itself, as in the case of Heineken beer, which ran the strapline: 'Heineken refreshes the parts other beers can't reach' and later trimmed it down to: 'Refreshingly Heineken'. The strapline or slogan will often appear alongside the logo, emphasising its role not just as a brand statement, but a corporate one as well.

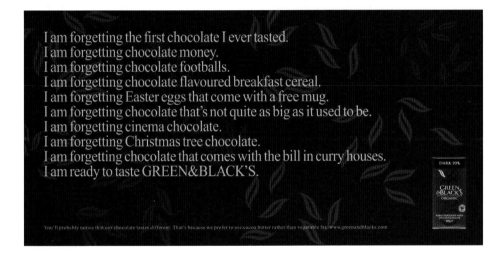

I am forgetting (above)
This copy-led ad for Green and Black's exclusive organic chocolate dismisses the inferior taste of other, cheaper chocolates.

Client: Green and Black's / Agency: Fallon London / Creative Directors: Richard Flintham and Andy McLeod / Creatives: Ed Edwards and Dave Masterman / Designer: James Townsend

Visualising the concept

Thumbnails and roughs

Working at small scale in thumbnail or rough sketches is a good starting point. Thumbnails, as the name indicates, are small hand-drawn sketches of your ideas that are sometimes accompanied by a written explanation. You may wish to produce a rough that is larger, however try not to make it bigger that A5, otherwise you may spend an unnecessary length of time trying to draw in detail. Focus in on the action and limit the background information to the bare necessities. In the early stages of idea generation you must get the idea down on paper quickly and with limited effort. Don't spend good idea generation time worrying about camera angles and layout – stop, pin the visual up on the wall and move on to the next thought. It is good practice to pin your ideas up on a wall – that way you can reflect on them during the day. Also, other people have the chance to view them and offer feedback.

Visualising your idea on paper is important, so that the creative director and account team can understand your concept simply and easily. If you aren't very good at drawing, don't worry – it's the quality of the idea that is important and you can get away with drawing stick people or describing the concept in words. Over time, you can develop better visualising techniques and remember, a good idea will show through a bad drawing.

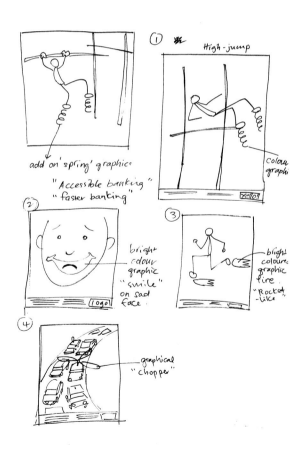

Thumbnails (right)

Generate ideas, and lots of them. Don't waste time attempting to draw beautiful pictures. If it helps, describe your ideas next to your thumbnail sketches.

Sketches by Alicia Wen-Hui Chong, lecturer at the Raffles Design Institute, Singapore

One-stroke visuals

The next stage is to produce 'one-stroke' visuals that progress the best and most promising of your thumbnail sketches. One-stroke visuals are black and white drawings that explain the concept in a simple and uncomplicated way – adding too much information or detail will detract from the impact of the central idea. At this stage the layout design is considered. The elements that are normally included are the visual, the headline (which should be written in and not typeset) the payoff or tag line, any body copy (which can be indicated by a series of wavy lines), and crucially the brand or product logo.

A variety of concepts are normally presented to the creative director and then later to the account team. At this point you may be asked to go away and develop one or more of the concepts further, which involves pushing the concept as far as it can go and testing its campaignability. Creative directors look for a big idea, which can be executed effortlessly across a variety of advertising media.

If the ideas need to be rendered up to a more finished standard, the larger agencies hire expert visualisers. These artists work from the art studio and have excellent drawing and magic marker skills, which allow them to produce slick visuals and storyboards almost effortlessly. Being able to produce good, legible black and white visuals is a skill worth developing, because in small and regional agencies the creative team will be required to be more self-reliant.

Simple visuals (below)

Keep your visuals simple, but do consider the layout design and the composition of your picture (e.g. landscape or portrait etc).

Sketches by Alicia Wen-Hui Chong, lecturer at the Raffles Design Institute, Singapore

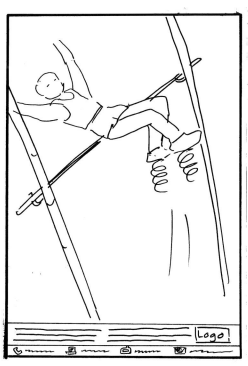

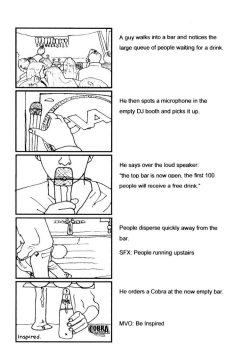

A guy walks into a bar and notices the large queue of people waiting for a drink.

He then spots a microphone in the empty DJ booth and picks it up.

He says over the loud speaker: "the top bar is now open, the first 100 people will receive a free drink."

People disperse quickly away from the bar.
SFX: People running upstairs

He orders a Cobra at the now empty bar.

MVO: Be Inspired

The storyboard and script

If you are planning a TV treatment as part of your campaign this is shown by a combination of a written script and a visual storyboard. The script is a written plan of the commercial, featuring a description of the setting, the action, words and dialogue, voice-overs, any sound, special effects and music/soundtrack. The creative team's initial storyboard visualises the key frames (the important ones which everything else stems from), and attempts to tell the story in 4–6 frames. The best storyboards show the progression of action in a simple and clear way, avoiding complex camera directions at this stage. The purpose of the storyboard is to explain the idea to the creative director and account team and over-elaborate directions may confuse the communication.

To assist in the production of a storyboard, art directors sometimes photograph each key frame with a digital camera and then, using a light box, trace over the action with a black pen. Written alongside these illustrated frames will be the words, audio and any description of the set or location. The commercial's director may also devise a more complex shooting storyboard or written treatment later on, once he or she has been briefed.

Sometimes an animated storyboard, an animatic, is used to 'sell' the concept to the client or for pre-testing purposes. A rostrum camera films the storyboard using simple camera movements and transformations, such as zooming in and out, pans, dissolves and cuts, to bring the storyboard to life.

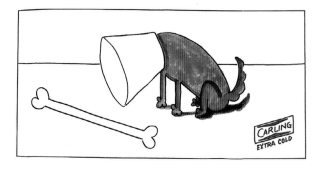

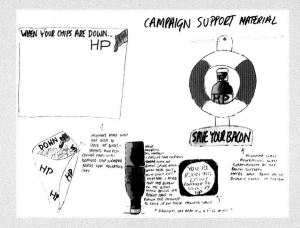

Presenting ideas to the client

The next stage is for the account/client services team (and possibly the creative team) to present the preferred concepts to the client. Depending on the client's level of visual literacy, they will be shown either as simple black and white, one-stroke visuals or highly finished visuals. Highly finished visuals normally mean that the headline and subheads (and sometimes body copy), are typeset and a magic marker visual or a stock photograph is used to illustrate the visual. This practice has the advantage of replicating the advertisement before it goes into production, but has the major disadvantage of limiting the artistic licence the art director and photographer/director/illustrator can employ when executing the concept. As Marie Voss, a creative at JWT London points out; 'Our visuals aren't finished at all. Often they're rough sketches. We normally just draw the logo on for the client. If you can't see the idea in a bad drawing it is probably not a good idea. If you can't draw it, just write next to it what it is supposed to be.' It has even been known for clients to be so impressed by the visual that they think it is the finished advertisement.

Dog rough (opposite, bottom)
Drawn in a cartoon style, this visual tells the story in a simple and uncomplicated way.

Art Director: Raymond Chan / Copywriter: Simon Cenamor

Cobra storyboard (opposite, top)
Sometimes photographing real life situations and then tracing over each frame with a black pen can create a highly effective storyboard.

Concept and execution: Sam Bowden and Neil Collins, students on the BA Advertising course at Southampton Solent University.

When your chips are down...Save your bacon (above)
Chris Spore developed this slick magic marker visual for a hypothetical HP Sauce campaign while at university.

Concept and execution: Chris Spore

Do it!

Try to produce a simple animatic from one of your storyboards.

Firstly, work out what camera movements and transitions you would like to include. You may have to increase the size of the storyboard frames (photocopying is a quick method), allowing you room to make the planned camera movements. Borrow a video camera and a tripod and create a very simple animatic.

CHAPTER 5
ART DIRECTION

Photography and illustration

Selecting the right execution for a print-based advertising campaign is an important part of the production process, and it is at this point that the concept comes to life. In many cases the very nature of the concept dictates which type of execution will be appropriate. The decision to use photography or illustration is based on what will achieve the purpose of the advertisement most effectively.

Photography versus illustration

Photography is widely regarded as 'real' and adds credibility to the message contained within the advertisement. The audience perceives a photograph as believable, as it can depict the product as it actually is and in the context of a 'real' environment. In the case of packaged goods, a photograph also fulfils the basic function of ensuring the reader knows what to look for on the shop shelf. Some advertisements show the product as a 'pack shot', which is separate to the main visual or displayed as an inset. This allows the art director to show the product at its very best, beautifully shot and in pristine condition. Photographing the product makes it a matter of fact. Executing the same visual by illustration could enter the realms of fantasy.

However, illustration is undoubtedly hugely versatile and offers the art director a variety of styles and genres to choose from, such as cartoon, photo-realism, airbrush, watercolour, collage and print making. Buying into a particular style of drawing can perfectly reflect the values of the product or brand being advertised and can be used across the various media that make up the campaign.

Commissioning photography does provide the art director with more control during this part of the production process. In consultation with the photographer, the art director can have input into the casting, the styling of the set and props, directing the shoot and may oversee any retouching or image manipulation. As with commissioning photography, illustrators are chosen because of their style and portfolio of work, and in the belief that they can add new dimensions to the concept. However, because there is a limited 'hands-on' role for the art director to play in the action, using an illustrator to execute the concept can be a difficult process. Briefing the illustrator or their agent thoroughly plays a major part in the success of the end result, because it may be several weeks before the finished artwork arrives back from the illustrator.

Vertigo (opposite, bottom)

The tables, cafetiere and cups in this ad were all shot in a studio. The cityscape and the flying ducks were later superimposed on to the image. This involved careful planning to ensure that all elements fitted perfectly.

Client: Gallaher Plc / Agency: Dorlands / Photographer: Keith Ramsden

Beer from the coast (opposite, top right)

Illustrated ads can be just as lively, colourful or evocative as photographic ones. These ads are attempting to convey a particular mood and atmosphere, which may have been more difficult to create using photography.

Client: Adnams Plc / Agency: SHOP / Illustrator: Christopher Wormell

Food photography (above)

Food photography is a specialist area of the advertising business. To prepare food and make it look good for the camera requires hired home economists. They cook and style the food, sometimes using ingenious tricks to achieve the very best look.

Soup: Client: BBC UK Food / Photographer: Andy Seymour
Chilli: Client: Blue Dragon / Photographer: Andy Seymour

CUT FOR YOU.

Digital image making

Some illustrators/photographers now use digital technology to create or modify their images, and this has blurred the traditional boundaries between illustration, graphic design, photography and printmaking, all of which are now collected together within the realm of image making. Being able to combine these disciplines has enabled the image maker to sample elements of popular culture ephemera and original, handcrafted artwork. Torn out magazine pictures, old bubble gum wrappers, concert tickets, photographs and original illustration can all be scanned. Then using software such as Photoshop, Illustrator and Freehand these images can be manipulated, enhanced, and colours altered until the desired effect is achieved. However there is still a need for craft, whether the artist starts off with a blank piece of paper or a blank screen.

Photo-manipulation and retouching

The evolution of the computer and specialist software has meant that digital manipulation and retouching techniques have made huge advances. Consequently photography and illustration have come closer together as a medium and visuals that in the past were only possible through illustration can now be achieved through combining a number of shots together then manipulating and retouching them. The photographer carefully plans and provide the various shots that make up the composition, so when combined and retouched, they work as one shot.

You're better off by bike
On short trips it's quicker and more convenient

MAYOR OF LONDON   tfl.gov.uk/cycling   Transport for London

Cut for you (opposite)
This brilliant collage using Levi's denim literally illustrates the 'cut for you' campaign concept.

Client: Levi Strauss do Brasil / Agency: Neogama BBH / Marketing Director Latin America: José Claudio Motta / Photographer: Bruno Cals/ Illustrator: Junior Lopes

Shift it (above)
Subtly altering familiar images to give them a different meaning is a good technique.

Client: Transport for London / Agency: M&C Saatchi / Creative Director: Graham Fink / Art Directors: Tiger Savage and Joe Miller / Writer: Paul Pickersgill / Photographer: Leon Steele

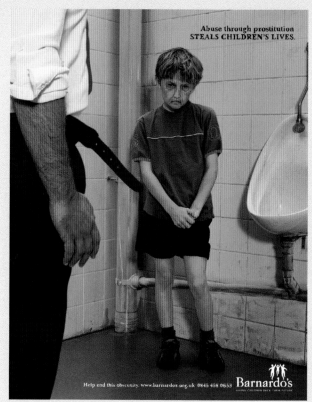

Barnado's sofa. Barnado's toilet. (this page)

These haunting visuals demonstrate how powerful photographic image manipulation can be when used on the right subject.

Client: Barnado's / Agency: Bartle Bogle Hegarty UK / Creative Directors: Alex Grieve and Adrian Rossi / Producer: Shelley Buick / Photographer: Phil Poynter / Creative Team: Ester Katrine Hjellum, Jon Robb, Adrian Rossi, Alex Grieve

The end of the question mark (this page)

These ads demonstrate the power of illustration to show an abstract and imaginary idea in a humorous and vibrant manner.

Client: IssueBits Ltd/Any Question Answered / Agency: SHOP / Illustrator: Adam Howling

THE END OF THE QUESTION MARK. Text any question to 63336 and have the answer within minutes.

THE END OF THE QUESTION MARK. Text any question to 63336 and have the answer within minutes.

The New Beetle Cabriolet.

The New Beetle Cabriolet.

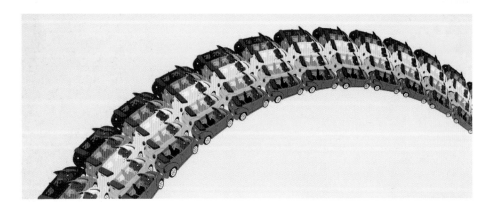

The New Beetle Cabriolet.

Bees. Butterflies. Rainbow. (this page)

Buying into a particular style of illustration gives this campaign a fresh and different look for the brand.

Client: Volkswagen UK / Agency: DDB London / Art Directors: Feargal Ballance, Jeremy Craigen, Lovisa Almgren / Copywriters: Dylan Harrison, Ewan Paterson, Ben Wade / Illustrator: Ian Bilby / Typographer: Peter Mould / Creative Directors: Jeremy Craigen, Ewan Paterson
Image supplied courtesy of the D&AD Global Awards (Art direction: Silver Nomination, 2005)

Art buying

The search for the right photographer begins with the creative team sifting through photographers' and agents' websites and viewing online portfolios of work. Photographic agents will represent some of the very best advertising and editorial photographers. Apart from showing their clients' work online, they also take the portfolios to the advertising agency for the creative teams and art buyers to view. This work varies quite dramatically, depending on the style or genre of photography required; lifestyle cars, fashion, food, landscape, architectural, reportage and portraiture are all catered for.

It is important for art directors to build up good relationships with their art suppliers, and this is especially true with photographers. They have the ability to produce a last minute shot that can 'save the day' for the agency. However the role of the freelance photographer has been undermined by the increased popularity of stock photography. Stock photography is bought or commissioned from photographers and can be used and reused for advertising and design purposes. Advertising agencies, publishers, web designers and graphic designers all use stock photography agencies to a greater or lesser extent. A major advantage of using stock over original photography is convenience; the client can search through databases of photographs and download a high resolution image without moving from their offices. Savings on the cost of hiring a photographer, models and props/set/location hire is also a major consideration for some clients. However, stock photography images may be familiar to your audience, if they have been used by other organisations. Commissioning well conceived and executed original photography will always have the creative edge because photographers can meet your requirements and fulfil your concept – or add to your concept through their own creativity.

With thousands of photographers and numerous photographers' and illustrators' agents, the creative team need some assistance in selecting the right person for the campaign. Many larger agencies employ art buyers who act as a link between the image suppliers and the agency.

Do it!

Take one of your most successful campaign concepts and plan a photographic shoot or illustration brief.

Firstly, research and select the most suitable photographer/illustrator for the job – bear in mind your concept and chosen style when considering suppliers. Conduct some background research and talk to advertising photographers, illustrators or agents to ask their opinion.

Mussels (right)
Being able to view different photographers' portfolios of work online has been an important development. This allows art directors the chance to view many portfolios before deciding on a shortlist for the job in hand.

Photographer: Patrice de Villiers / Agent: Carolyn Trayler Agency

The photographic shoot

Once the decision has been made to use an original photograph as the advertisement's visual, and a photographer has been commissioned, the production process begins in earnest. This is an important phase in the development of the advertising campaign; poorly planned and executed photography can dramatically weaken a good idea.

Preparation

First, the photographer needs to be briefed thoroughly. Reviewing the art director's visual of the advertisement is a good starting point. Irrespective of whether the photographic shoot will take place in a studio or on location, the various elements that make up the shot need to be sourced and agreed upon by the art director and photographer.

Depending on the subject of the shot, the casting/selection of the models to be featured in the shot may need to be organised. This process normally involves using the services of model agencies, which supply models and actors for all types of shoots including fashion, lifestyle or portraiture. The correct style and size of clothing also has to be purchased or hired for the shoot.

If a location needs to be chosen it may be necessary to visit the site with the photographer before the shoot, in order to check its suitability. Specialist location hunters may also be commissioned to find the perfect location for the shot.

Sometimes it is easier to build a small set in a studio than go on location. If this is the case then model makers and set builders may need to be briefed. Studio lighting is much more manageable than that on location. Using studios also reduces the need to transport equipment to the shoot. When planning a studio shoot, the right backdrops and props need to be selected and sourced. Specialists such as stylists and make-up artists can be commissioned to assist on the shoot.

The big day

With the planning and preparation in place, it is important that the art director attends the photographic shoot. On the day the art director's primary task is to make sure that all the plans are properly executed and to answer any queries and solve any problems that arise.

If the shoot is being shot on film the art director will need to check any preliminary tests. Before shooting, film photographers will normally shoot tests on Polaroid film. If the shoot is digital, any test shots can be downloaded on to a computer for the art director to view.

It is vital the art director ensures that the shot is in proportion to the selected media size. A portrait shot does not naturally lend itself to a 48-sheet poster format! Variations may need to be shot to facilitate different sizes of media. The art director needs to be sure that everything is covered, but without adding extra shots.

If the shot is not working as planned, the art director will need to work with the photographer to improve it; maybe a change of angle or closer framing is required. Whatever happens, the shot needs to be 'in the bag' by the end of the shoot.

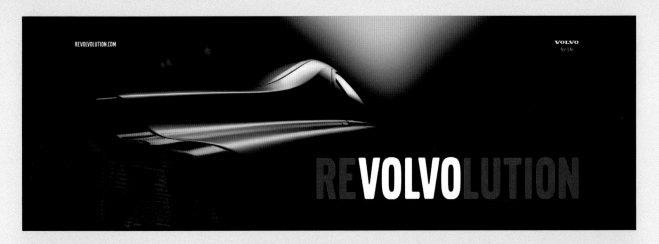

Mercedes-Benz SL

It's better than it looks (bottom)

This Mercedes ad was shot on a very simple background that enhanced the shape of the car. The ad was used as an outdoor poster campaign.

Client: DaimlerChrysler / Agency: Leo Burnett London / Art Director: Matt Gooden / Copywriter: Ben Walker / Photographer: Chris Bailey

Revolvolution (top)

This is one of a series of ads created as a pre-launch campaign for the Volvo S60. The ads were used in the press and as outdoor posters. It was unusual to see a campaign that did not show the whole car clearly and says a lot for Volvo's confidence in their product and in the creativity of the images.

Client: Volvo / Agency: Messner Vetere, New York / Creative Director: Guy Seese / Photographer: Chris Bailey

Art Deco lady (opposite)

This image was used in a corporate brochure for a company based in a famous Art Deco building. This 'one shot' used a model cast by a model agency and a hand-painted backdrop created by set builders.

Photographer: Keith Ramsden

Carousel (above)

This photograph for BAA promoting special offers on flights was shot as a two-part composite. The luggage carousel was photographed at Stansted airport, and the money image was superimposed later.

Client: BAA / Photographer: Keith Ramsden

Do it!

Look at your portfolio and select a campaign that is suitable for a photographic execution. Research and plan as though you were really going to commission a photographer and run the campaign.

Plan the logistics and practicalities of your photoshoot. Do you need to scout for locations or will your shoot be studio-based? Do you need to cast models? If so, what kind of clothes should they wear and how would you direct them? Will you need any kind of set, props or particular weather or light conditions?

What style and format of artwork do you need, and what type of photographer would be appropriate? Look at photographers' and agents' portfolios online to identify suitable photographers.

Crafting the campaign look

Once the basic campaign concept for the advertisement has been formulated and agreed by the client, it's down to the creative team to coordinate its execution. In traditional creative partnerships, the copywriter will write any body copy so that the message is conveyed in a punchy and memorable way, using the correct tone of voice to evoke the right mood or provoke the desired reaction. The art director will be responsible for 'crafting' the advertisements – making sure that they look visually strong and have a consistency of layout and composition across the campaign. Crucially, they must also exude and reflect the brand values.

Layout and composition

Part of the process of art directing press and print advertising involves laying out the various elements of the advertisement into a composition that is not only pleasing to the eye, but also supports the message. The components of the advertisement normally consist of the visual (if any), which may be executed through photography, illustration or a graphic, the headline, body copy and the brand or company logo.

The best art directors keep the layout and composition simple allowing the idea to shine through. Although well considered, clever art direction is something we can admire, it is not something that should get in the way of communication or distract the reader from the advertising message itself. In other words, the art direction should help communication by making the message easier to understand. If it tries to 'show itself off' in a way that is not relevant or appropriate to the message or the concept, then it often ends up obstructing communication by distracting the reader from the message. It is equally true that the best art direction in the world will not make a poor idea any stronger.

So what should the art director be trying to achieve in terms of layout and composition? As with most aspects of creative advertising, there are no hard and fast rules, only a few guidelines and principles, and even those need to be challenged sometimes. It is only once you know these guidelines and principles that you can start working on when and where and how to break them.

Peas. Corn. Crumpet. (this page)

Good art direction shouldn't distract the audience from the message. A simple visual treatment can make a great idea even more powerful.

Client: Lurpak / Agency: DDB / Art Director: Justin Tindall / Copywriter: Adam Tucker / Typographer: Peter Mould / Photographer: James Day

Big soup (this page)

These ads use an obvious idea that is literally based on the soup's brand name. Don't dismiss the most obvious and simplistic ideas!

Client: Heinz / Agency: Leo Burnett

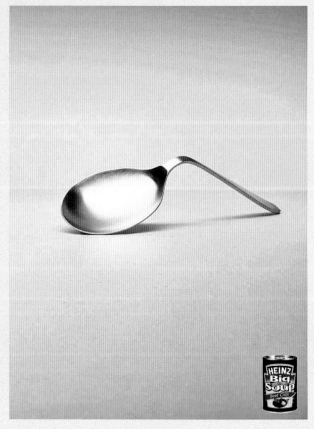

Keep it simple

Generally speaking, the look of the page should be kept simple and uncluttered. There will be a temptation to cram the page with everything that is relevant to the product. The art director must decide what is important and then edit it down to the simplest visual image, while still providing the reader with enough visual clues and references to understand the message. If the art director fails to do this, it is likely that the advertisement will be too 'busy' and provide no clear focal point or pathway for the reader's eye. Ultimately, the reader should be led through a desired sequence of images and text, taking him or her on a seamless journey from picture and headline to the final sentence of the body copy.

In order to achieve this a good layout should start with a strong focal picture or image, which will not only draw the attention of the reader to the advertisement, but will also work well with the headline. If there is more than one image on the same page, then they should not compete with one another for audience attention.

Ideally, a strong layout will contain a dominant picture, or in the absence of a picture (as in the case of a 'headline-only' advertisement), a dominant piece of typography. Any other images included within the advertisement may be small inset pictures, annotated with captions perhaps, but the key principle is to keep things as simple as possible. If the message is clear and strong with a single image, then the art director should not be tempted to add too much visual material, as the impact of the advertisement may be diluted.

Hellmann's Extra Light (this page)

This simple execution uses a pack shot with a difference.

Client: Hellmans / Agency: Lowe London / Creative Director: Ed Morris, Photographer: Mike Parsons

THE BIG ISSUE FOUNDATION. SUPPORT FOR ADDICTION, MENTAL ILLNESS, RE-EMPLOYMENT AND ACCOMMODATION. THINK BIGGER.

WORK THIS OUT. A PERSON DIAGNOSED WITH A MENTAL DISORDER SLEEPS IN A DOORWAY. A PERSON WHO'S COMPLETELY SANE WALKS RIGHT PAST THEM EVERY MORNING.

THE BIG ISSUE FOUNDATION. SUPPORT FOR ADDICTION, MENTAL ILLNESS, RE-EMPLOYMENT AND ACCOMMODATION. THINK BIGGER.

ARE YOU HAPPY TO LIVE IN A WORLD THAT FINES ONE PERSON FOR LETTING THEIR DOG DEFECATE ON THE STREET BUT ALLOWS ANOTHER TO SLEEP THERE INDEFINITELY?

Think bigger (opposite and above)
This series of ads demonstrates how sensitive art direction allied to an unusual layout and sympathetic typography can make a campaign work really effectively.

Client: The Big Issue Foundation / Agency: TBWA / Art Director: Paul Belford / Copywriter: Nigel Roberts

Small but tough. Polo. VW

Make the image work harder

Although the copywriter is responsible for writing the words, the art director should ensure that the visual relationship between the text and elements such as the image, headline, strapline, logo and any other graphic details that make up the printed advertisement achieve maximum synergy and impact.

The art director might consider cropping in close to the object being featured. If it is a refrigerator for instance, does the whole fridge and half of the kitchen need to be shown? How much of the fridge needs to be shown and what clues can be provided by the context? For instance, it might be possible to show just a section of the fridge door, with the handle and a few brightly coloured fridge magnets. These elements are quite distinctive and still communicate the message, but in a more focused, simple and clear way. There is another reason for keeping the image simple; simpler images are easier to recall.

Small but tough (above)

By using a common tone of voice across all campaigns, Volkswagen has ensured that the single messages they try to deliver about each individual model – in this case Polo's sturdiness – are ultimately common Volkswagen engineering values.

Client: Volkswagen / Agency: DDB / Art Director: Nick Allsop / Copywriter: Simon Veksner / Typographer: Peter Mould / Illustrator: Paul Slater www.centralillustration.com

Be here (opposite and overleaf)

The image shouldn't just illustrate the headline. In these ads it is the combination of the strong image, headline and Penguin logo that work together to complete the story. Each of these three components do their part of the job to communicate.

Client: Penguin Books / Agency: Mustoes / Art Director: Dean Hunt / Copywriter: Simon Hipwell. / Photography: Magnum Photographers / Typography: Unreal

be here

Combining typography and image

There are certain visual combinations that work very well together. For example, a dramatic headline in a bold typographic style that 'shouts' from the page often complements a more subdued image. The opposite is also true; if the image is a bold one that screams from the page, then a headline that 'whispers' is very effective. That way, the headline and the image complement rather than compete against each other for the audience's attention.

On occasion, however, challenging some of these basic principles can work to great creative effect. For instance, if the team is trying to create a particular retrospective visual style in their advertisement, many of the visual treatments that are considered ineffective in a contemporary sense may be relevant and appropriate to the advertising message.

Think small (below)

The image and the typography should complement, not compete with, each other.

Client: Volkswagen / Agency: DDB New York / Art Director: Helmut Krone / Copywriter: Julian Koenig / Photographer: Wingate Paine

Creating a visual surprise

Good art direction involves more than just a sense of good layout and aesthetics – it involves the ability to present the reader with a visual surprise. Imagine for example that you are working on a campaign promoting performance swimwear and your visual idea is a photograph of a swimmer in a swimming pool. It is an image that most of us are familiar with. The trick is to have the photograph shot in a way that is very different to the image that most people would be familiar with or expect. Typically, the familiar image would probably be a photograph taken from the side of the swimming pool as a medium or close-up shot of the swimmer travelling across your field of vision, or even a more dynamic close-up image of the swimmer surfacing for air as he or she swims towards the camera. Both of these images are perfectly acceptable, and indeed we see them every day in advertising and news media. However, it is because we see these images every day that they have become familiar and 'expected'. They suffer from what has been described as the 'SOS (same old shot) syndrome'.

The task of the art director is to confound the expectations of the readers; to present the familiar, but in an unfamiliar way. In fact the images that create most impact on the audience, are often those, which at first may present some kind of visual ambiguity or conundrum. It is when the audience makes the connection and understands the image that impact is achieved. When an ordinary object is presented in an extraordinary way, it becomes a more interesting image.

The headline that accompanies the image will also affect the impact and way by which the image is interpreted. However, the notion that the audience has to 'get' the idea immediately, no longer applies to every case. Today's audiences are much more media-literate and tend to have a greater capacity to decode advertising messages. There is also the 'puzzle' element to consider. We all tend to enjoy solving puzzles, finding solutions and working out the answers. If we have had to work a little bit harder to get the message, we are more likely to remember that message. Allowing the audience to make their own discoveries allows advertisers the opportunity to engage their potential consumers in a way that involves them in the brand message and helps to promote loyalty to that brand.

A conker, noticed after
a visit to the Tate.
Minds open from 10am.
TateGallery

A conker (above)
Good art direction often involves showing a familiar object or scene in an unfamiliar way – making the usual unusual!

Client: Tate Gallery / Agency: BDDP.GGT / Art Director: Paul Belford / Copywriter: Nigel Roberts

Lewisham –Tower of London 30 mins
It's on your doorstep

southeastern
www.setrains.co.uk
Text LEW to 84118 for Days Out ideas

Bromley South – Buckingham Palace 27 mins
It's on your doorstep

southeastern
www.setrains.co.uk
Text BROMLEY to 84118 for Days Out ideas

It's on your doorstep (this page)
These posters give the reader a visual surprise and conundrum to work out.
Why is a royal guard standing guard over a country cottage?

Client: South Eastern Trains / Agency: Rapier / Creative Director: John
Townshend / Art Director: Tony Clements / Copywriter: Hugo Bone / Comms
Planner: Henry Nash / Photographer: Nick Meek / Agent: Siobhan Squire /
Producer: Sue Odell / Location Finder: Big Fish

Biggest for sport (opposite)
Manipulated and retouched photographs, or illustrations?

Client: The Times / Agency: Rainey Kelly Campbell Roalfe/Y&R / Creative
Directors: Jerry Hollins and Mike Boles / Art Director: Andy Clough /
Copywriter: Richard McGrann / Photographer: Nick Meek

BIGGEST FOR SPORT
THE LARGEST SPORT SECTION OF ANY DAILY PAPER

www.timesonline.co.uk

THE TIMES

BIGGEST FOR SPORT
THE LARGEST SPORT SECTION OF ANY DAILY PAPER

www.timesonline.co.uk

THE TIMES

Beer from the coast
(this page and opposite)

These illustrations perfectly evoke the Suffolk seaside, where Adnams is brewed, and draw inspiration from British Rail posters from the 1930s.

Client: Adnams Plc / Agency: SHOP / Illustrator: Christopher Wormell

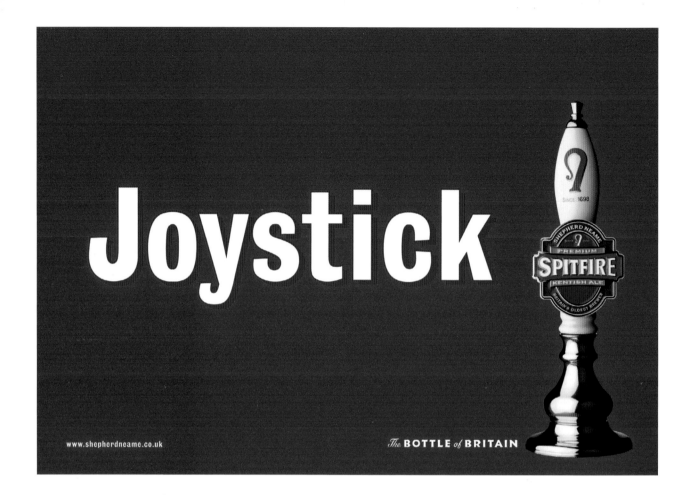

The bottle of Britain (above)

This ad plays jokingly with the brand name of the beer, and its connection with the Second World War. The brand name is pivotal to the campaign idea.

Client: Shepherd Neame / Agency: RPM3 / Creative Director: Russell Wailes / Creative team: Ian Pittams and Denis Williams

Nikon (this page)

These beautifully shot Nikon ads could have been taken by the camera they are selling! When you have a good-looking product, make sure the photography is of the highest quality.

Client: Nikon / Art Director: Nick Scott / Copywriter: Paul Cardwell / Photographer: Mike Parsons

Typography

In this context, typography can be described as the selection and use of typefaces to convey a message in the best way possible. Understanding how important typography is to the success of a campaign is key to effective art direction; the legibility and suitability of the chosen typeface(s) can make or break the successful communication of the message. The nature of working with type has changed dramatically since the introduction of the personal computer in the 1980s and in particular the development of the WYSIWYG (what you see is what you get) graphic user interface (GUI). Previously, typographers, trained over many years, worked to very strict rules and controlled – or very possibly limited – the opportunities for experimentation within typography. The many 'rules' of typography originated during the rather inflexible days of metal type and while it is important to have an understanding of the basics of typography, good art directors are prepared to take risks, to challenge preconceptions and, in many cases, quite simply have fun with type to communicate the desired message.

Typeface selection

With the proliferation of typefaces in contemporary use it is vital for the art director to make some fairly rapid decisions about the relevant style of typeface(s) for the client. Consider the appropriateness of the following selections:

Ye Olde Tea Shoppe
Byte Size Computers

The choice of typeface will create a first impression that can be hard to alter, however good the campaign is. The choice of typeface has to reflect the nature of the brand, product or service and examining a brand's logo can provide vital clues as to the direction the typography should take. Choosing a typeface with a sympathetic 'tone of voice' is also important to the communication of the advertisement. If the tone is incorrect, then the headline will lose some of its impact and meaning.

As with so many areas of design, it is important to keep typography simple. The majority of art directors often work with a very limited selection of typefaces – usually their favourites, which have worked well for them in the past. However, typefaces are being designed and revised on a regular basis so an awareness of the latest developments and styles is useful. If an advertisement contains headline, body and a strapline copy, then it is advisable to avoid using several different typefaces as these may create visual confusion, an alternative is to use different weights from the same font family.

The typefaces selected should be appropriate for the medium or media that the campaign is to be developed in. A typeface that works for a billboard campaign may be totally unsuitable for a television or online campaign. There is little point in using a fine serif typeface (i.e. a typeface with a flourish on the finishing stroke of the letter) on something that is to be viewed on-screen, as the resolution will not always cope with the subtlety of the font's design. Consider how difficult it is to read some of the credits at the end of a film even on a large cinema screen. Similarly, it can be risky to use a small point, fine serif typeface on a printed medium if it is to be reversed out of a colour background. If a campaign covers both print and on-screen media then the typefaces used are a vital consideration.

SICK AND TIRED OF PEOPLE SLEEPING ROUGH IN YOUR AREA? I SHOULDN'T WORRY, THEIR AVERAGE LIFE EXPECTANCY IS ONLY 42.

WHY HELP A HOMELESS, EX-SERVICEMAN FORCED ONTO THE STREET THROUGH DEPRESSION WHEN YOU THINK HE'S A DIRTY THIEVING HEROIN ADDICT WITH A FLAT AROUND THE CORNER?

Think bigger (this page)

These well-crafted ads break the rules. Body copy set in capitals and positioned at the top of the layout and a headline looking cramped – and, horror, no logo!

Client: The Big Issue Foundation / Agency: TBWA / Art Director: Paul Belford / Copywriter: Nigel Roberts

Fentimans (this page)

Leith London commissioned top typographer David Wakefield to faithfully produce these Victorian-influenced posters using period illustrations, promoting the authenticity of Fentimans real lemonade and ginger ale. Victorian-style wooden printing blocks were made up of all the elements, apart from the bottle shot.

Client: Fentimans / Agency: Leith London / Art Director: John Messum / Copywriters: Simon Bere and Richard Evans

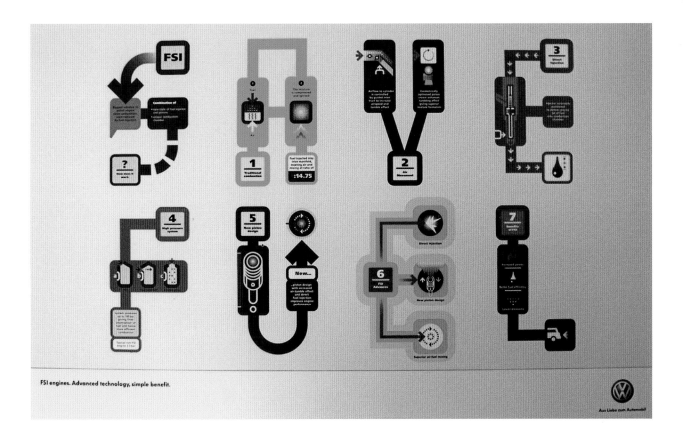

Save fuel. Smooth shifts (this page)

These specialist car magazine ads talked directly to petrol heads (car enthusiasts), about how technologically advanced Volkswagen cars are. The typographic style illustration allowed the creative team to talk in a human way about advanced technology.

Client: Volkswagen UK / Agency: DDB London / Typographer: Spencer Lawrence / Art Director: Nick Allsop / Copywriter: Simon Veksner / Illustrators: Peter Grundy, Arthur Mount, Russell Cobb / Creative Director: Jeremy Craigen
Image supplied courtesy of the D&AD Global Awards (Typography for Advertising Campaigns/Silver Nomination, 2005)

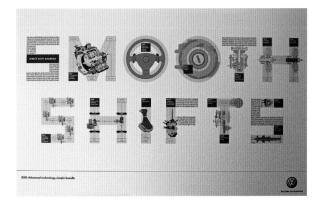

Be creative, yet concise

It is all too easy to be rather traditional and often downright boring when planning the typography of a campaign. There are, of course, many times when carefully considered type needs to fit in with the existing values of the client, but this does not mean that conventions can't be challenged. If a campaign has a number of prominent words then it might be appropriate to replace one or two of the characters in the words with an image or object that represents that character. Perhaps the typography becomes the image – integrating words and pictures into an illustration.

Whatever your approach, remember to keep text short. Simply cutting down the number of words used in a campaign can work to great effect. Clarity and simplicity often make a message more powerful and allow the type that is used a greater impact.

Bless you Bisto. Thank you Mr Kipling. Thanks Robertson's. (below and opposite)
Sometimes using the typography to create a 'visual' adds an extra dimension to the communication.

Client: Ariel / Agency: Saatchi & Saatchi / Art Director: Andrew Clarke / Copywriter: Ross Ludwig

The text on the banana reads:

Have you ever written on a banana in biro? It's crazy but it works like a dream. You wish all writing could be this way. It flows. It's smooth. It's sensual. You get the urge to write poems; sonnets; odes to lilies. A strongly worded letter of complaint is impossible. It makes you realise that everything can be improved. That even the familiar can be looked at in a new light. And that imagination is more powerful than knowledge. Do you believe in the power of dreams? HONDA

Honda banana (this page)

This handwritten calligraphy style works very effectively.

Client: Honda UK / Agency: Wieden + Kennedy London / Creatives: Chris Groom and Richard Russell / Photographer: Paul Zak

Crash (opposite)

Sometimes type can be used to create an image. This ad for The Guardian is particularly successful in showing a train crash visually through text.

Client: The Guardian / Agency: DBB / Art Directors/Copywriters: Feargal Ballance and Dylan Harrison / Typographer: Kevin Clarke

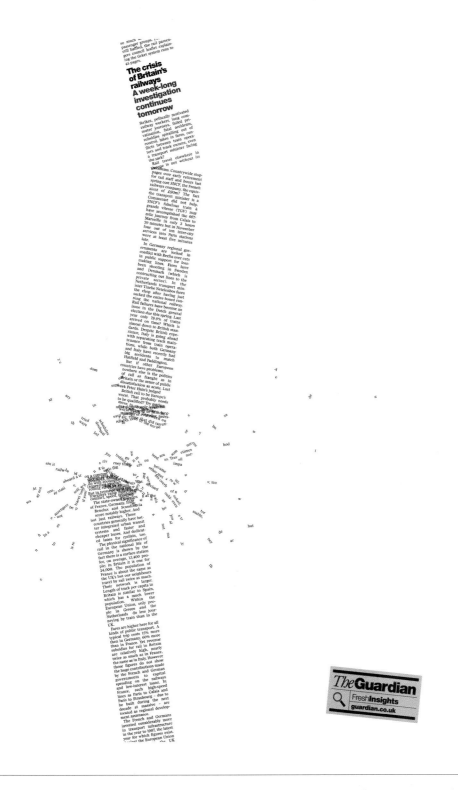

Do it!

Using only typography, create and illustrate an image of a tree. Make the words you use relevant to the subject matter.

A picture is worth a thousand words

Purely image-based advertising campaigns are nothing new. Benson and Hedges cigarette advertising from the 1970s and Benetton posters from the early 1990s demonstrate how effective this genre is. The importance of the image is even more relevant in today's global marketplace where brands have to transcend cultural boundaries. Now language is no longer a barrier, as long as the visual communicates the right message.

The cream of Manchester: Dartboard. Melted ice cream. Fuel gauge. (this page and opposite)
This award-winning Boddingtons campaign uses only a visual and a logo on its press and poster ads. Creating a campaign that has so much longevity is difficult to achieve without a strong, central idea such as this.

Client: Boddingtons Cream of Manchester / Agency: Bartle Bogle Hegarty UK / Creative Team: Jo Moore and Simon Robinson / Photographer: David Gill / Model making: Gavin Lindsay

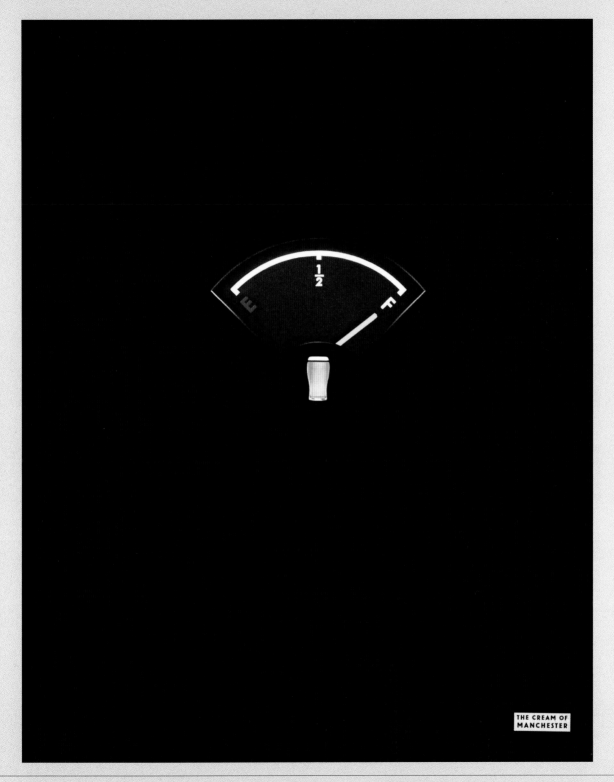

THE CREAM OF
MANCHESTER

Less need for copy

It could be no coincidence that the popularity of no-copy advertising has spread alongside the increased use of the internet. The internet allows for further details about a product or service to be read at leisure, removing the need for long copy press advertisements. The internet's 24-hour marketplace provides consumers with an interactive brochure to leaf through at their leisure. A few clicks of the mouse allows them to view the latest television commercial or take a virtual tour around the product.

The visual tells the whole story

The very best non-copy advertisements work quite simply because they don't actually need copy. Instead they communicate instantly and use a campaign idea that has longevity. The creative team must attempt to make the communication a simple as possible – some image-based advertisements are less successful because they ask the receiver to work too hard to decipher an over-complicated visual, when a few words of explanation would assist the communication.

NEW **GUINNESS**. EXTRA COLD

NEW **GUINNESS**. EXTRA COLD

In your creative team, work
on this brief for a DIY
superstore – to promote
their products to a female
audience. Research has
confirmed that women
have become important
buyers of DIY products
and gardening equipment.

Do it!

In your creative team, work
on this brief for a DIY
superstore – to promote
their products to a female
audience. Research has
confirmed that women
have become important
buyers of DIY products
and gardening equipment.

Your task is to produce an
image-led campaign for
women's magazines that
targets potential female
customers. The tone of the
ads should be modern and
vibrant, promoting an
enjoyable consumer
experience.

Stand out from the crowd

It is widely accepted that today's consumers are more sophisticated and visually literate than ever
before, which makes them far more selective about the type of image they consume. Sometimes a
single, dynamic visual that stands out can say far more about the brand than a range of product
shots. An intriguing, mysterious, or even shocking visual, which allows the viewer to complete the
message, makes it more memorable because it is interactive and engaging.

**Guinness Extra Cold: Iceberg. Lolly. Tap. Fan. (opposite and
this page)**
These Guinness Extra Cold ads use the iconic Guinness glass symbol in
simple illustrations to portray 'extra cold' in various ways.

Client: Guinness / Agency: Abbott Mead Vickers BBDO Ltd.

CHAPTER 6
THE FUTURE OF ADVERTISING

A changing industry

There is little doubt that the future holds radical changes in several aspects of the advertising industry. Broadly speaking, these can be defined as the media; the message; the market; and both the advertisers and agencies. The evolution of advertising will therefore be centred upon the relationship between each of these components. Although it is impossible for anyone to predict the future of advertising in any certain terms, it is possible to look at past trends and the potential of current and future technology, to make some informed guesses at the shape of things to come.

The media

The form and nature of advertising is likely to be in a constant state of change as it adapts and re-invents itself to accommodate new technology and the fresh demands and requirements of an amorphous marketplace. Historically, the popularity of one advertising medium over another has always been part of the general ebb and flow caused by the impact of new technology and market demands. There is no reason to suspect that this trend will cease as we look forward. In the near future we could see less use of network television and a greater use of direct marketing communication as a vehicle for advertising. The fragmentation and complexity of the media today is forcing advertisers and their agencies to look at new, unconventional forms of media together with fresh and imaginative ways of using old media.

While traditional advertising media such as press, radio, television and posters still play an important part in the media mix, a combination of new technology and creative thinking has opened up a range of new media opportunities. The proliferation of the internet, digital media and mobile phone technology has not only increased the channels of communication, it has provided new opportunities for advertisers to engage with their audiences interactively. The growth in direct marketing is also set to escalate, as access to the internet increases and interactive digital television continues to develop, allowing a greater sense of 'one-to-one' communication between advertisers and their audiences. As the popularity of such media has increased, so too has their tendency to converge on each other. Perhaps the most dramatic example of this is the development of WebTV, which combines the benefits of internet and TV access in a single package.

The use of new media may not be confined to just the internet and digital media. It may also involve an increase in the use of media that have not previously been fully exploited for advertising. A good example of this is the growing use of 'ambient advertising' (see Ambient media, p.28), which often involves the use of media in new and unusual ways in order to grab attention amid the deluge of more conventional and traditional forms of advertising that we are used to seeing.

The market

As markets continue to become more global and multicultural, advertisers and their agencies are faced with new challenges. Economic growth and new technology have in effect made the world a smaller place. As a result, there is now more pressure on advertising to be culturally transportable. A single campaign may have to work across a variety of different national markets and culturally diverse audiences.

In response to this, consumers themselves are beginning to demand more from the products they buy and the services they use. They are becoming less likely to respond to communication that does not address them on a personal level. All signs seem to indicate that one future consumer market trend will be the demand for more direct marketing communication that engages consumers on a one-to-one level. Already, many advertisers are starting to seek out niche markets and many of them are beginning to offer specific brands or services to specific target groups. Advances in technology have enabled advertisers to access sophisticated software and databases which enable more accurate targeting of individual consumers. This in turn helps to facilitate a more personal relationship between the consumer and the brand. Even the products themselves can often be personalised with the provision of accessories and other 'add-ons' that allow consumers to get closer to the brand.

The message

Placing emphasis upon the quality of communication could be a way of counteracting the postmodern consumer's natural instinct to filter out advertising messages and reject the 'hard-sell'. The fundamental principle of the advertisement informing or entertaining its audience will still apply, but in the future the sales pitch will be less obvious. Individual interest in a particular product or brand, or the desire to purchase it, will be generated in a more subtle way. Consumers will not only have the desire, but also the ability to 'shut out' advertising messages. New strategies will be needed to target audiences that seek different types of relationships with the brands that they buy, and have different expectations of the companies that own those brands.

The way in which cultural codes change and evolve with the passage of time calls for constant re-evaluation of how advertisers communicate with their audiences. At one level, advertisers will need to be aware of shifts in societal values. Organisations are already under pressure to demonstrate a social conscience and care for the environment, for example.

Advertisers will also need to be sensitive to shifting conventions and styles in both design and language. What is fashionable and appealing one year may look or sound outdated the next, and in the worst case scenario, may result in the brand losing credibility and share of the market.

The agencies and the creatives

The advertising industry is increasingly faced with the dilemma of choosing between generalisation or specialisation. While the capacity to provide services, media expertise and creativity across a broad range of areas and cultures remains an asset for most international agencies, there is also a call for agencies that have more specialist skills and knowledge.

One way that many agencies are tackling this dilemma is through greater, more flexible integration of services. The last few decades have witnessed dramatic changes in the way that advertising agencies operate. Many of them have acquired other companies offering specialist communication services, such as new media or public relations. In many cases, the advertising agency is the major stakeholder within a larger communication group that offers a wide and varied range of services through its member companies. This has not only enabled agencies to extend their reach, it has also provided them with the opportunity to put together teams of individuals whose combined specialist skills and expertise is most appropriate for the project at hand. This, in turn, enables better co-ordination and synergy of marketing communication; a process that has been termed Integrated Marketing Communications (IMC).

Industry perspectives

'What do you think will be the most prominent changes we'll see in the industry over the next 10 years?'

Graham Fink
Creative Director, M&C Saatchi

'The future of advertising is an exciting world. Mainly because of the uncertainty and fear surrounding new media and technological advances. I translate that as a wonderful opportunity. Tabula Rasa. A brand spanking new canvas. Nietzsche said it best with, "one needs chaos in one, in order to create a dancing star". Absolutely.

'How perfectly wondrous that out of this confused state, new and exciting ideas will emerge. Fresh thinking is needed like never before. The brave will triumph for sure.
I can't wait.'

Nigel Clifton
Creative Director, EHS Brann

'The future of advertising is destined to be [about] more personal and more direct communication. With the media channels in our hands – like iPods, XDAs and souped-up mobile phones, advertising will head in two directions. There'll be bigger, grander, more entertaining and content-driven campaigns that embrace every channel and connect with everybody. And there'll be more discrete, personal, direct communication driven by data and understanding of each and every one of us and the way we interact with companies and products. The internet and other digital media will drive the future of advertising without any question. So it's not a question of "if" that's going to happen, but "when".'

Robert Pott
Formerly with Y&R Group. Now Creative Director for Three 'Virtual' Agencies

'What is the future of advertising? As long as there are brands, there will always be advertising. Dear old Maslov will continue to have his needs and as religion – the ultimate brand – has shown us, we're a species that loves a good story and a ritual.

'So while people are prepared to believe that a tick can make you more sporty, an anagram of an obscenity emblazoned across your chest will make you more attractive and that waiting ages for your pint to be poured really is a benefit, then advertising will remain a great business to be in. As for the future of advertising agencies, I'm not sure if that is so rosy. The 'doyens' I'm certain will always occupy their West End ivory towers but the irrepressible rise of the Mac and the web has meant that mere mortals can now network from home.

'Everyone can now be a designer and typographer. Ideas are no longer king, but mere servants to execution. I believe it is the era of the virtual agency where overheads (including the odd chairman's Ferrari) are sacrificed for a more flexible, proactive and cost-effective way of working… good news for clients, not so good for the restaurants of Soho.'

APPENDIX

Conclusion

The fundamental principles covered in this book will provide an excellent foundation for your own understanding of the business and enable you to approach your study of this discipline in a well-informed, critical way.

Having grasped the fundamentals, we hope that you will be able to use the examples, exercises and theories provided in this book as a starting point from which to explore your own creative potential. Remember though, that it is about *origination*, not imitation. If you set out to copy great work, you will never produce anything original, so instead be inspired by the examples provided. Ask yourself: 'What is it that makes that idea, or that campaign work?'. Then set out to create something that is even better! Good luck.

Advertising is an exciting field to work in and the industry is constantly changing to provide new challenges and creative problems to solve. The true test of creativity is the ability to adapt to change, and consistently find new and original solutions to the client's brief. Advertising is likely to play a crucial role in marketing products and services for the foreseeable future, but the opportunities offered by new technology and media provide a much broader canvas for advertisers, their agencies and creative teams. The most creative solutions will find innovative and integrated ways to use the media to reinforce brand values and communicate clearly to a modern, media-literate audience.

In this book, we have focused on what are traditionally seen as the more creative aspects of the advertising business, with the emphasis on conceptualising and crafting the advertisements themselves. However, in reality, all aspects of the advertising business involve the ability to think creatively and solve problems. Whether your own interest is in ideas generation, media planning, production or the strategic account management side of the business, advertising offers a wide array of opportunities and limitless creative possibilities.

Illustrations (opposite)
Be inspired by the examples provided. Ask yourself: 'What is it that makes that idea, or that campaign work?'

Full details and credits for these images are on pages 35, 79, 92 and 158.

Student resources

D&AD (British Design and Art Direction)
Founded in 1962, D&AD is one of the foremost organisations representing the creative industries in the UK. As well as providing resources for practitioners, D&AD offers a wealth of valuable benefits and resources for students and postgraduates alike, ranging from the prestigious student award schemes and competitions, to training workshops, lectures, professional contacts and the facility to exhibit work online and at their annual 'New Blood' exhibition.

Membership of D&AD is now available to individual students as well as their respective colleges and courses. The D&AD *Annual* and *Showreel* showcase the best design and advertising around and is an invaluable source of inspiration for both aspiring creatives and current practitioners.

D&AD, 9 Graphite Square, Vauxhall Walk, London, SE11 5EE, UK
T: +44 (0) 20 7840 1111
F: +44 (0) 7840 0840
W: www.dandad.org

Campaign
Published weekly, Campaign is generally recognised as the trade newspaper for the advertising industry. It provides up-to-date information on what is happening in the business, together with reviews of new campaigns, feature articles, topical commentary from leading practitioners and recruitment pages.

Brand Republic, 174 Hammersmith Road, London, W6 7JP, UK
T:+ 44 (0) 20 8606 7500
E: subscriptions@haynet.com
W: www.brandrepublic.com/magazines/campaign

Young Creatives Network (YCN)
The YCN is an organisation involved in promoting new creative talent and provides a number of valuable resources for students through member colleges. These include a student award scheme and an annual publication showcasing the best emerging creative talent from courses across the country, together with live briefs and features about key industry topics. The YCN is free to join online, and members have full access to all online content.

YCN, First Floor, 181 Cannon Street Road, London, E1 2LX, UK
T: +44 (0) 20 7702 0700
F: +44 (0) 20 7702 9869
E: info@ycnonline.com
W: www.ycnonline.com

The Advertising Standards Authority (ASA)
Since 1961, the ASA, together with the Committee of Advertising Practice (CAP) has been responsible for administering the self-regulation of non-broadcast advertising in the UK. In 2004, both of these organisations entered a partnership with the regulatory body Ofcom and are now also responsible for the regulation of TV and radio commercials. The ASA judges advertisements in response to complaints from the public and business, and can require misleading or offensive ads to be changed or withdrawn.

As well as administering a student awards scheme, the ASA offers free and accessible classroom resources that provide an insight into how advertising regulation works. These resources include examples of ads the ASA has adjudicated on and activities for classwork and student research.

ASA, Mid City Place, 71 High Holborn, London, WC1V 6QT, UK
T: +44 (0) 20 7492 2222
F: +44 (0) 20 7242 3696
E: enquiries@asa.org.uk
W: www.asa.org.uk

NABS

NABS offers help and support to individuals working in advertising, design, direct marketing, media sales, public relations and sales promotion.

NABS provides a range of services for all those in the marketing communications industry. These include careers advisors, a research library, 'getting started' publications and a careers room, which is fully equipped with computers, scanner, faxes, phones and internet access. NABS also have agency contact lists, show-reels and credentials, a comprehensive library of trade press, directories and access to industry sites. They offer face-to-face consultations together with advice on writing a CV, putting your portfolio together and interview skills.

All of these resources are completely free. NABS also offers weekly crits (sessions to critique work), as well as placement opportunities, links with headhunters, and help with finding a creative partner through initiatives such as their Lonely Hearts Book Club and the Portfolio Bootcamp.

NABS, 91a Berwick Street, London, W1F 0NE, UK
T: +44 (0) 20 7292 7330
E: nabs@nabs.org.uk
W: www.nabs.org.uk

OpenAd.net

OpenAd.net is a global online marketplace for advertising, marketing and design ideas. The ideas are submitted by creatives; who may be established practitioners or students, or indeed anyone with a good idea. As well as submitting random, unbranded ideas, creatives have the opportunity to work on live briefs, and to pitch for business. Interested companies can register as 'buyers' and have the option to buy the rights to use any of the ideas or concepts submitted by the creatives. OpenAd.net employs a number of online processes to register, safeguard and protect the ideas submitted.

T: +44 (0) 20 7290 2711
E: jo@openad.net
W: www.openad.net

IPA (Institute of Practitioners in Advertising)

The IPA is the trade body and professional institute for 250 leading agencies in the UK's advertising, media and marketing communications industries, covering the creative, digital media, direct marketing, healthcare, media, outdoor, sales, promotion and sponsorship sectors.

The IPA is committed to best practice in graduate recruitment to the marketing communications industry and offer a wide range of advice on applications, placements and member agency vacancies as well as comprehensive recruitment opportunities through IPA Jobs Online. This resource allows students to post their CVs online as well as look at job vacancies.

The IPA, 44 Belgrave Square, London, SW1X 8QT, UK
T: + 44 (0) 20 7235 7020
F: + 44 (0) 20 7245 9904
E: info@ipa.co.uk
W: www.ipa.co.uk

The Institute of Direct Marketing (IDM)

The IDM represents the direct marketing industry. This industry body helps students get that first foot in the 'marketing door'. Those looking for work placements or job opportunities can get in touch with prospective employers through their jobs noticeboard. The IDM offers a number of on-the-job training schemes, which are actively supported by most agencies in the industry.

IDM, 1 Park Road, Teddington, Middlesex, TW11 0AR, UK
T: +44 (0) 20 8977 5705
F: +44 (0) 20 8943 2535
E: enquiries@theidm.com
W: www.theidm.com

Marketing Communications Consultants Association (MCCA)

MCCA is a trade body for the UK's marketing communications agencies. The MCCA has developed several professional development services aimed at helping people who are looking for a career in a marketing communications agency. They publish graduate vacancies and offer a programme to help agencies recruit graduates direct from university.

MCCA, 3–4 Bentinck Street, London, W1U 2EE, UK
T: + 44 (0) 20 7935 3434
F: + 44 (0) 20 7935 6464
E: info@mcca.org.uk
W: www.mcca.org.uk

The European Association of Communications Agencies (EACA)

The European Association of Communications Agencies (EACA) is a Brussels-based organisation whose mission is to represent full-service advertising and media agencies and agency associations in Europe.

EACA aims to promote honest, effective advertising, high professional standards, and awareness of the contribution of advertising in a free market economy and to encourage close co-operation between agencies, advertisers and media in European advertising bodies.

EACA, 152 Blvd. Brand Whitlock, B-1200 Brussels, Belgium
T: +32 2 740 07 10
F: +32 2 740 07 17
W: www.eaca.be

The European Advertising Standards Alliance (EASA)

The European Advertising Standards Alliance (EASA) is a non-profit organisation based in Brussels. EASA brings together national advertising self-regulatory organisations (SROs) and organisations representing the advertising industry in Europe.

The EASA is, on behalf of the advertising industry, the single authoritative voice on advertising self-regulation issues and promotes high ethical standards in commercial communications by means of effective self-regulation, while being mindful of national differences of culture, legal and commercial practice.

EASA, 10a rue de la Pépinière, B-1000 Brussels, Belgium
T: +32 2 513 78 06
F: +32 2 513 28 61
E: library@easa-alliance.org
W: www.easa-alliance.org

The International Advertising Association (IAA)

The International Advertising Association is a one-of-a-kind strategic partnership that champions the common interests of all the disciplines across the full spectrum of marketing communications – from advertisers to media companies to agencies to direct marketing firms – as well as individual practitioners.

IAA World Service Center, 521 Fifth Avenue, Suite 1807, New York, NY 10175, USA
T: + 001 212 557 1133
F: + 001 212 983 0455
E: iaa@iaaglobal.org
W: www.iaaglobal.org

The Incorporated Society of British Advertisers (UK)

The ISBA is the representative body on all aspects of marketing communications for some 380 leading UK advertisers, whose combined spend on marketing communications is over £10 billion per annum.

Membership includes companies in all areas of business. The single factor binding ISBA members together is their reliance on advertising and commercial communications to communicate with consumers.

ISBA, Langham House, 1b Portland Place, London, W1B 1PN, UK
T: +44 (0) 20 7291 9020
F: +44 (0) 20 7291 9030
W: www.isba.org.uk

The History of Advertising Trust Archive

The History of Advertising Trust (HAT) Archive was established in the UK in 1974 by a small group of individuals who believed that the best of UK advertising should be preserved for posterity. In 1978 HAT was established as an educational research trust and a registered UK charity. Its initial brief was to encourage and sponsor the study of all aspects of the growth and development of advertising. The HAT Archive is now probably the largest archive in its field in the world.

The History of Advertising Trust Archive, HAT House, 12 Raveningham Centre, Raveningham Centre, Raveningham, Norwich, NR14 6NU, UK
T: +44 (0) 1508 548 623
F: +44 (0) 1508 548 478
E: archive@hatads.org.uk
W: www.hatads.org

The World Federation of Advertisers (WFA)

The WFA is the only global organisation representing the common interests of marketers. The WFA membership is a unique, worldwide network of 55 National Advertiser Associations on five continents and over 40 of the world's top 100 advertisers.

The WFA incorporates more than 10,000 businesses operating in a broad spectrum of sectors at national, regional and global level. This network represents around 90% of global marketing communications, totaling almost US$ 700 billion annually.

The WFA, 120 Avenue Louise, 1050 Brussels, Belgium
T: +32 2 502 57 40
F: +32 2 502 56 66
E: info@wfanet.org
W: www.wfanet.org

The Fink Tank

This website was conceived by award winning creative director Graham Fink and offers aspiring creative teams the chance to work on new creative briefs, exchange ideas, meet new partners and attend workshops.

Thefinktank, 25 Lexington Street, London, W1F 9AG, UK
T: +44 (0) 20 7851 0851
F: +44 (0) 20 7439 0001
E: info@thefinktank.com
W: www.thefinktank.com

The Art Directors Club

The Art Directors Club encourages students to explore the field of visual communications with year-round educational events, scholarships, and exhibitions. Their career workshops teach local high school students the fundamentals of the trade and encourage them to apply to art school and enter the profession. Their student portfolio reviews provide an opportunity for graduating college students across the US to meet with creatives from the top ad agencies, design studios, and I-shops to review their work.

The Art Directors Club, 106 West 29th Street New York, NY 10001, USA
T: +001 212 643 1440
E: info@adcglobal.org
W: www.adcglobal.org

The One Club

The One Club for Art and Copy is a non-profit organisation dedicated to promoting the craft of advertising. Founded in 1975, The One Club has approximately 1000 members, including copywriters and art directors. As part of its mission to promote high standards of creative excellence, The One Club produces the advertising industry's most prestigious awards program, The One Show. Judged by a panel of the advertising industry's elite creative directors, this annual event acknowledges excellence in art direction and copywriting in a variety of categories, including television, radio, newspapers, magazines, billboards and public service announcements. The coveted One Show 'Gold Pencils' are highly regarded in the advertising world.

The One Club for Art & Copy, 21 East 26th Street New York, NY, 10010, USA
T: 001 212 979 1900
E: info@oneclub.org
W: www.oneclub.org

The Internet Advertising Bureau (IAB)

The Internet Advertising Bureau, is the trade association for the internet marketing industry and, more specifically, online advertising. Students can find out more about online advertising, which is the most exciting and fastest growing advertising medium, by visiting their website.

IAB, Ingram House, 13–15 John Adam Street, London, WC2N 6LU, UK
T: +44 (0) 20 7886 8282
E: info@iabuk.net
W: www.iabuk.net

Thanks

Ken, Nik and Caroline would like to thank all of the agencies and individual practitioners who have helped with this book or whose work we have featured. In particular: Nigel Clifton, Alicia Chong, Graham Fink, Phil Hawks, Nick Morris, Bob Pott, Seb Royce and Colin Stone for their valuable contributions; Chris Bailey, Keith Ramsden and Andy Seymour for supplying their photographs for publication; Roger Cayless and Giles Ecott at TMP and Matt Lawton at Lawton for visual material; Carolyn Cummings-Osmond of Southampton Solent University for inspiration on the student exercises for the copywriting section and Mandy Wheeler of Punch It Up (www.punchitup.co.uk) for the student exercises at the end of the radio section of this book.

Also a special thanks to the D&AD who have provided us with support and material for the book and the many students past and present who have helped and inspired us, in particular Sam Bowden, Simon Cenamor, Neil Collins, Nick Cooper, David Rose and Chris Spore. Finally, our thanks to Brian Morris, Leafy Robinson, Renée Last and Sarah Jameson at AVA Publishing for letting this book see the light of day.

Ken

I would like to thank my Mum and sister, Linda, for their continued support, plus a big thanks to my co-authors Nik and Caroline, without whom this project would not have happened.

Nik

I would like to thank my family: my wife Tracy and my children, Kieran and Sarah, and my mother Trudi for support over the years – lots of love to all of you. My co-authors, Caroline and Ken – well done guys. Finally, special thanks to Simon Barwick, who gave me my first break in advertising and became an important influence in those formative years.

Caroline

Thank you to Ken and Nik for asking me to contribute to this book and for welcoming me into the team. Thanks also to all my students for their input and inspiration and finally a huge thank you to John, Julia and Hannah – you're the best!